Catholic Leadership

Lessons from Jesus and a Faithful Centurion

R.D. Miksa

NEPPERHAN PRESS, LLC
YONKERS, NY

Copyright © R.D. Miksa, 2011

All rights reserved. No part of this book may be reproduced or transmitted in any form or by any means, electronic or mechanical, including photocopying, recording, or by any information storage and retrieval system, without written permission from the author, except for the inclusion of brief quotations in a review.

Published by Nepperhan Press, LLC
P.O. Box 1448, Yonkers, NY 10702
nepperhan@optonline.net
nepperhan.com

Printed in the United States of America

Library of Congress Control Number: 2011921077

ISBN 978-0-9829904-2-1

Cover art was licensed from Publitek, Inc.

To my wife Jessica,
whose love and dedication
during my writing of this book
truly exemplified the Christian virtues
of patience and perseverance.

CONTENTS

INTRODUCTION *A FAITHFUL CENTURION*	*1*
CHAPTER 1 *WHAT IS LEADERSHIP?*	*12*
CHAPTER 2 *FOLLOWING A CARPENTER?*	*30*
CHAPTER 3 *BUT JESUS AND THE MILIARY?*	*35*
CHAPTER 4 *BE A LEADER AND LEAD BY EXAMPLE*	*50*

CHAPTER 5
  GATHER INTELLIGENCE, STAY CURRENT,
  AND REMAIN AWARE
	62

CHAPTER 6 *BETTER TO GIVE THAN TO RECEIVE*	*73*

CHAPTER 7
  COMMUNICATE STRATEGICALLY AND
  KEEP YOUR FOLLOWERS INFORMED
	80

CHAPTER 8
  GUIDE, TEACH, AND TRAIN YOUR
  FOLLOWERS AND YOURSELF
	93

CHAPTER 9
  ALWAYS SHOW INTEREST, CONCERN,
  AND IMPARTIALITY
	101

CHAPTER 10
  KNOW WHEN AND HOW TO BE A
  FOLLOWER
	108

CHAPTER 11
  BE MORE THAN A FRIEND, LESS THAN A
  FRIEND, AND SOMETIMES JUST A FRIEND   *116*

CHAPTER 12
  BE PREPARED TO TAKE A STAND AND IF
  NECESSARY STAND ALONE   *127*

CHAPTER 13
  BECOME THE LEADERSHIP PRINCIPLES   *135*

CHAPTER 14
  CATHOLICISM AND LEADERSHIP STYLES   *142*

CHAPTER 15
  THE ACTIVE STRENGTH OF LOVE   *150*

CHAPTER 16
  THE PASSIVE POWER OF FAITH   *165*

CHAPTER 17
  ARE YOU A CATHOLIC LEADER?   *174*

INTRODUCTION
A FAITHFUL CENTURION

And when Jesus entered Capernaum, a centurion came to Him, imploring Him, and saying, "Lord, my servant is lying paralyzed at home, fearfully tormented." Jesus said to him, "I will come and heal him." But the centurion said, "Lord, I am not worthy for You to come under my roof, but just say the word, and my servant will be healed. For I also am a man under authority, with soldiers under me; and I say to this one, 'Go!' and he goes, and to another, 'Come!' and he comes, and to my slave, 'Do this!' and he does it." Now when Jesus heard this, He marveled and said to those who were following, "Truly I say to you, I have not found such great faith with anyone in Israel...." And Jesus said to the centurion, "Go; it shall be done for you as you have believed." And the servant was healed that very moment (Matthew 8:5-10, 13, NASB).

"One minute!" The words cut into my earpiece, overpowering every other sound and snapping me into focus. "Final equipment check!" my Commanding Officer bellowed through the radio, making certain that no one mistook the instruction's importance or urgency. "Get ready to move on my command!"

The order had been given; finally, *it was time.*

"One minute," I yelled, passing the warning along to my awaiting troops. My voice rose above the endless rumble of a dozen idling jeeps and armored fighting vehicles, their exhausts kicking up hazy dust clouds as their metal hulks stood framed against a blood-red horizon and the setting Afghan sun. My thirty-man platoon had already checked their equipment a dozen times, but they instinctively checked it again, reacting as they had been trained to do.

In less than sixty seconds, our convoy would roll out the camp gate, passing through its ever-vigilant machine gun pillboxes and watchtowers, to conduct the mission that had been set before us: raiding the urban compound of a high-ranking enemy commander. It was a mission that would very likely be as dangerous as it was important. So far our snipers, who had been covertly observing the site for the past twenty-four hours, had seen a number of men traveling back and forth in the area but had gained no firm intelligence on who might be in the compound or just how many people might be there. To make matters worse, both women and children were expected at the location, a fact that would add a whole new dimension to our operation.

Analyzing these last pieces of information as I stood beside my jeep, the lead vehicle of the entire convoy, I looked at the men under my charge. They sat stoically in their vehicles, a rock-hard determination visible on every single face. But behind that look was also a silent expectation, an expectation that if they upheld their end of our bargain, and I knew that they would, then I would be expected to uphold mine. Their job was to fight our battles and my job was to lead them. Their very lives rested on the decisions that I would make, and my life would rest on how well they carried out those decisions. That was our unvoiced agreement. That was our unwritten contract. They were my soldiers and I was their commander, and I was expected to fulfill and embody all the unspoken characteristics that such a serious role demanded, for in this pact there would be no second chances or new decisions. My leadership, or lack thereof, would not cost money or career advancement or social standing, but blood. Its success or failure would be determined in lives: the lives of my men, the lives of the enemy, and potentially, the lives of innocent civilians. The fate of all these people would rest not only on the decisions that I would make, but also on who I truly was as a leader.

Considering all this, and fully realizing that the ultimate price might be paid by someone else for any misstep on *my* behalf, there was nothing else for me to do but reach for the small gold cross that hung from my neck. Underneath an inch of Kevlar plating, ammunition, and other gear, I could feel the cross subtly pressed against my chest. A gift from my wife, given to me just before shipping out for my tour to Afghanistan, I had not taken it off since. And as my fingers traced its outline, a quiet whisper escaped my lips, forming a short prayer that sprang forth involuntarily.

"God, protect my men."

So quiet were the words that even I barely heard them, but since that very moment they have been forever etched into my memory. Everything that I could have done to prepare myself and my men for what lay ahead had been done. If we were not ready now, we would never be. There was no turning back. Yet no more than a few seconds before we rolled out onto the busy streets to fulfill our mission, a strange realization came over me: at no time in my entire life had I needed my leadership, *as well as my Catholic faith,* more than I did in that instant. And at no time in my entire life was I more certain that I had both.

It is extraordinary that at such crucial moments, when calamity is staring us in the face, our faith can bring forth both a serene calm and a solid steadfastness precisely when the opposite might be expected. So it was with me, for my Catholic faith had never been as firm as it had been while the last fragments of that solitary minute ticked away. Such a certainty of faith was not, however, to be mistaken for a naïve belief that my platoon and I would be safe from danger or that no harm would befall us. Rather, it was the *ultimate* confidence provided by my stalwart faith that had suddenly become so certain and firm. It was a certainty both in Him above and in my men below, a certainty that we were truly ready for the task ahead and that everything would occur as it should occur. Having trained alongside my soldiers for so many hours, days, and months, I had developed a type of faith in them that deeply mirrored a religious one, for just as those who believe must ultimately place their fate in the hands of a higher power, so too must a soldier place his fate in the hands of his comrades. And as is the case with certainty and faith, it is also during the most crucial moments of clarity that we discover whether or not we truly possess leadership. In one flash of honest insight, our personal doubts or our inflated egos disappear, and we can truly acknowledge whether or not we are leaders, in more than just name, to the people that depend on us. I had cursed, sweat, and fought with my soldiers, and in the instant before I turned away from them to do a final check of my own equipment, I *knew* that I was their leader. The years of instruction and preparation and training in all facets of leadership had culminated in this personal realization; but in that same moment of clarity, I also grasped another aspect of my leadership.

Of all the various descriptors that one can add to leadership, be it "authoritarian" leadership or "transformational" leadership or "participative" leadership, I fit none of these. The only leadership classification that I could honestly place myself into was not even recognized as a valid classification, for I was a Christian, and more specifically, a *Catholic* leader. Indeed, I realized that I was *best* classified as a Catholic leader—if I can be excused the pride inherent in such a statement—because the one thing that I most certainly did was to always serve my soldiers before I served myself. I still commanded them and ordered them and held them under my authority, but in my heart I knew—and they knew this as well—that I always placed them first. I was a leader that my men would follow because I had always sought to place their needs in a higher priority than my own. I would always wash their feet before I washed my own, so to speak, just as Jesus had done (John 13:1-17).

Both during and after our deployment, many of my soldiers would tell me that I was one of the very best officers they had served with, and that they would have stood behind me regardless of my rank or authority. They followed me because they wished to, not because they had to. And if I could claim any credit for such an achievement, it would rest heavily on the shoulders of my Catholic faith, for without the formative lessons that Catholicism gave me, such leadership would not have been possible.

So I was a leader. And I realized this fact as I stepped into my jeep and stared at the sinking sun, its last rays illuminating the rocky mountain-tops that surrounded the city. Perhaps, I thought, in my own small way, I was a modern "Faithful Centurion," or at least one that was striving to be faithful. In fact, perhaps that singular story of Jesus and the faithful Centurion, one of true faith and deep concern for those in your charge, summed up my entire experience as a leader. Perhaps I truly was a *Catholic* leader. With that last thought, my driver popped the clutch and our jeep rolled out the camp gate, the rest of the convoy locked, loaded, and rumbling behind us as we set forth to fulfill the mission ahead.

This book is the completion of that mission. It is the completion of a journey I started the moment I experienced those key revelations just a few seconds before heading out the camp gate. It is a creation that stemmed from the leadership lessons that I learned, and the understanding that I gained, while serving in Afghanistan and throughout my military career. It is a book built upon the understanding that my leadership ultimately rests upon my Catholic faith, and the understanding that my Catholic faith was truly appreciated only after I had been required to lead others. Without a doubt, the success of my personal leadership depended wholeheartedly on the application of the principles, teachings, and morals inherent in Catholicism, while a true understanding of that same Catholicism only arose after being placed in a position of critical leadership. All my years as a military leader were inseparably, but subtly, interwoven with my years as a Catholic. And it is precisely by merging these two seemingly divergent, but all-consuming aspects of my person, that we arrive at the core purpose of this work.

Everything contained within this volume has been written with only one goal in mind: to aid you in embodying *true* leadership. What is critical to recognize, however, is that I did not state that this book was necessarily aimed at making you a *Catholic* leader, for the Catholic faith is not a necessary prerequisite for leadership. However, what I will illustrate is that true leadership stems from Catholic and Christian principles, regardless of whether or not we call them "Christian," and that these principles are embodied in the life, ministry, and leadership of Jesus Christ—the most successful leader in the history of human civilization. It is, therefore, by analyzing the teachings and example of Jesus, with an eye focused on leadership, that we will be able to draw forth the principles that can transform us into real leaders. So, while the Catholic faith is certainly not a prerequisite for leadership, the guiding foundations of leadership parallel those of Catholicism, and thus true leadership is synonymous with Catholic leadership.

CATHOLIC LEADERSHIP

Now, it must be understood that everyone is a leader, whether he is conscious of this fact or not. At some point in his life, every single individual will be called upon to stand at the forefront of those behind him and lead. Whether it is a teacher instructing her class, a parent raising his children, a community member guiding her fellow citizens, or a military general commanding his armies, at some stage in our lives we will all be called upon to lead in our own unique way. As such, this book has value for all people regardless of profession or position, for it can be used by all individuals to substantially enhance their own leadership skills. It is, however, specifically targeted for a select group of leaders.

It is aimed at those leaders that exist on a precipice, a precipice where their very leadership is inseparably linked to their own survival and the survival of the organization that they lead. These are the types of leaders whose continuing existence is the main proof of their successful leadership. Such is the leadership required in a military environment, where the leader's survival is wholly dependent on the very leadership that he provides to his men. And such was the leadership of the earliest founders of Christianity, where the "innocence of a dove" (Matthew 10:16) and the "shrewdness of a serpent" (Matthew 10:16) were the foundations upon which the faith survived through persecutions and trials. In modern arenas, such leadership can be seen in entrepreneurs that form the backbone of their growing business; community managers that act as stewards for society at large; the organizers of charities that provide vital services to those less fortunate; and religious mentors that guide those persons that seek out their counsel—to only name a few. Indeed, the personal leadership of individuals in these positions forms the cornerstone upon which their entire organization might stand or fall. It is for these individuals that this book was written.

At this point, and having read these last few lines, you may believe that the knowledge contained in this book is no longer useful for you. You may believe that because you no longer fit the specific type of leader that this book is written for, it no longer applies to you. This would be a mistake. For just as every human being will be a leader in some area or field during his or her life, every human being will also, at some point, be standing on a leadership precipice, where his very survival is at stake. Whether it is a family crisis, or a professional disaster, or a severe organizational blunder, everyone will be placed in situations that are dire, and thus *everyone* will need the leadership lessons taught in this book. So read on, as this book truly does apply to all.

With all this in mind, therefore, we must ask ourselves the question: How will this lofty aim of providing the key to real leadership be accomplished? How will a subject as diverse, intricate, and challenging as leadership be distilled into a few simple pages?

The method that will be employed is a simple, but highly effective one. The vast number of leadership lessons gleaned from my personal experience will be compressed into ten core leadership *principles* in order to provide you with a fundamental understanding of leadership that will apply itself to any situation. Although it may seem strange to presume that a topic as complex as leadership can be broken down into only ten principles, it is appropriate to remember that Jesus handily distilled His entire ministry into two key commandments: to love God and to love one's neighbor. These two instructions have the power to apply themselves to any circumstance and they also form the root from which all the other commandments grow. While there can be no argument that it is extremely difficult to truly exemplify these two commandments in daily life, it is certainly not hard to understand them. In much the same way, while actually *becoming* a leader is without a doubt truly difficult, understanding the foundations upon which leadership is built is not. In addition to providing the ten core aspects of leadership, this work will also illustrate how an understanding of those principles naturally translates into an embodiment of two specific leadership *styles* that every Catholic leader will need to employ in order to cope with different subordinates and different situations.

It must be absolutely clear, however, that abstract principles, concepts, and theories will not stand alone in this book, for it was only through experience that these principles were first discovered and formulated. It is, therefore, only through the examination of these experiences that the ten leadership principles can be properly understood. To that effect, each of the presented leadership ideas will be illustrated not only through an example from my own military experience, but also with examples found in the life and ministry of Jesus Christ. The employment of this technique will show both that these core leadership principles are timeless and that they supersede individual circumstance; they truly apply regardless of time, place, or leadership position. Indeed, the very fact that the leadership of Jesus can still be so incredibly effective in our modern era is a testament to the timelessness and permanence of true leadership.

Now, I understand that time is a precious commodity—which may make you wonder why you should take the time to read this book—but it must be reinforced that enhancing our leadership is vital precisely because leadership is both a universal function of society and a universal necessity that is crucial to every aspect of that same society. Leadership forms such a critical aspect of our daily lives, even if only as an undercurrent of our day-to-day activities, that it deserves serious attention and time. Solid leadership will improve an individual's, and a group's, attitude, cohesion, commitment, dedication, discipline, effectiveness, efficiency, integrity, morale, productivity, and reputation, along with the development of a multitude of other positive traits. An improvement in our leadership will naturally lead to an improvement in every other aspect of our lives. No fancy statistics, quotes, or anecdotes are needed to substantiate the absolute criticality of leadership for any organization. Any person simply has to pause for a moment of reflection to easily realize that every group, no matter how large or small, places someone at the tip of their spear, someone who guides them, someone who speaks for them, and ultimately someone who leads them. With this in mind, it is critical to remember that at the end of all calculations, the time spent improving one's leadership will pay itself back tenfold. And therefore, in much the same manner, the time spent reading this book will pay itself back tenfold.

In closing, it would be inappropriate of me not to mention my own personal motivations in putting pen to paper and creating this work. First, I wrote this book because I truly love the two topics that it combines: leadership and Catholicism. Second, I wrote this book because I wished to make a small contribution to those that are striving to become leaders. Finally, I wrote this book because I honestly believe it can help all leaders. Yet, while those three reasons are important, at my core I really wrote this book because after over a decade of leading others, being led, and watching others lead, I *know* that the leadership principles contained in these pages work! I know that they will work and I know that they will improve the leadership of anyone that honestly strives to employ and embody them. So while I readily admit that I am in no way unique or exceptional, I believe that this book is. It will wed two seemingly contradictory examples, the leadership of Jesus and the leadership of a military officer, into a seamless guide that works for all leaders, regardless of circumstance or position. And although I am certain that most readers are likely quite skeptical at this early stage as to how well this union will be achieved, I would nevertheless like to invite you to dive in and join me now in this quest to discover the principles of *true* leadership.

CHAPTER 1
WHAT IS LEADERSHIP?

FUNNY. HUMOROUS. Even ridiculous. These sentiments were, arguably, the only ones that could and *should* have been present in my soldiers the first day they met me. For how could it not be so? Imagine that you, a veteran soldier with a number of overseas deployments to the worst places in the world and years of military experience under your belt, were suddenly told that a twenty-something-just-graduated university student would be put in charge of you and thirty other hardened soldiers. Indeed, not only would he be in charge of you, but he would have professional authority over you and you would be under his command. Forget even imagining this from a military sense, but just think of your own profession, whatever that might be.

Imagine that the person who should have just started at the bottom of your organization's totem pole, was suddenly placed at its top. Or that the boyfriend that your daughter just brought home from college—who you are gnashing your teeth about—was suddenly your boss, making decisions that affected you day in and day out. Or, to approach it from a more Catholic perspective, imagine that a newly arrived parish priest, still wet behind the ears, suddenly deemed himself both capable and worthy to be the spiritual leader, guide, and shepherd to the parish's most senior pastors. In light of these imaginings, perhaps "ridiculous" does not even come close to expressing the proper sentiment that you would feel at such a situation. But this is exactly the state of affairs that my soldiers found themselves in when they met me, one of the newest and youngest officers to have just arrived at the military unit. And incidentally, this first meeting between my men and myself took place just a few weeks after they had returned from a demanding overseas combat deployment, making their perception of me that much more severe and penetrating.

Indeed, the footfalls from my combat boots sounded loud as they came down on the concrete floor all those years ago; I can still remember them now. And when I walked into the platoon common room, over thirty pairs of eyes stared me down, some friendly, although many not so much. I remember introducing myself and making some kind of speech. But most of all, I remember closing with the words, "I will always strive to have my actions speak louder than my words, both concerning my general attitude towards you as well as specifically concerning my leadership of all of you." Happily, for many of my men, they saw the truth of these words in the days, months, and years that followed.

Yet why is any of this important? Why is speaking about leadership in the abstract, rather than the practical, important? The reason for this is that while the idea of leadership seems to many people to be such a straightforward issue that it needs neither explanation nor elaboration, it is *not*. Understanding both what leadership is in the theoretical sense and understanding how leadership should be defined in unambiguous distinction to the sub-elements involved in leading—which are too often mistaken for leadership itself—is a vital requirement that needs completion before we can tackle the leadership principles themselves. And in order to achieve this clear distinction and understanding, it is necessary to address three key issues and how they are inter-related: management, authority, and leadership.

Management

From a Catholic perspective, and based not only on Catholic teachings but also on simple common sense, it is clear that the family unit is the most basic, universal, and vital form of group, thus necessitating the most basic, universal, and vital form of leader: the parent. Yet I am quite certain that it would not take you long to reflect upon a family that is known to you where leadership is largely absent (and if you yourself are part of such a family, then this book is both a necessity and a key resource for you to resolve that particular familial issue).

Now, this is not to say that such a family is disorganized. Indeed, many such families are highly organized, always punctual, and always have all their activities quite well coordinated. At the same time, however, such families and their parents simply take their children to and fro, from one activity to another, losing their focus and changing their personal pursuits yearly, if not monthly. They seem, to use a sailing analogy, to put every effort into where they are going, but let the changing winds decide what their ultimate destination will be. The same could be said for many other organizations as well, from the very largest to the smallest. And thus, it is precisely from these latter facts that the particular distinction between the idea of management and the idea of leadership, so often misunderstood, can be properly appreciated. For it is quite possible to be an organized, punctual, and coordinated manager *without* being a leader whatsoever, but it is impossible to be a true leader without also being a manager.

Unlike managing, which simply entails the management of resources and personnel, leadership is more. Leadership requires the creation of a vision, whereas management just requires the maintenance of that vision. Leadership requires choosing a direction, whereas management just requires staying the course. Leadership requires the formation of rules and methods of conduct, whereas management just requires the enforcement of them. Leadership requires laying out a plan of action, whereas management just requires the coordination of it. Indeed, being a leader means presenting and developing new ideas, new ways of completing tasks, and new ways of thinking; being a manager does not.

First and foremost, being a manager requires maintaining the status quo. In contrast, at its core, being a leader means both setting the course of action for a group and then starting to move that group towards the desired goal, while a manager just holds to and preserves the course that the leader has already set out. So while you *cannot* be a good leader without simultaneously being a good manager, you *can* be a good manager without being a leader. Too often this distinction is confused, creating managers who think they are actually being leaders. And all the while, the subordinates of these so-called leaders know that they are actually only managers, and thus the subordinates act according to this underwritten understanding, meaning that they act as if they have no real leader, which greatly weakens overall group effectiveness and cohesion.

This difference between leadership and management is, therefore, a crucial one, and it is one that needs to be both clearly and firmly understood if the remainder of this book is to have its desired effect. It is also a distinction that you must personally reflect upon if you are currently in a leadership position, or are about to embark on one, in order to ensure that you are not simply managing when you should be leading. So remember, as a leader you must always strive to lead, not just to manage.

Authority

"I am in charge here!" These words, venomously, aggressively, and unnecessarily spewed out, have almost certainly been heard by everyone from at least one foam-spitting boss—who likely seemed to think that he was near divine in his authority. Indeed, it is a line most likely heard alongside these other ones: "You will obey my instructions!" or "I have the power here!" or "I am the one who tells people what to do around here!" However, in contrast to this overbearing superior, there also exists the boss who is timid, indecisive, and ineffectual, yet who simultaneously holds all the authority necessary to make decisions and select the courses of action mandated for the remainder of the group. It is almost unavoidable that at least one such "leader," if not both, has been encountered by all of you who are reading these words. It is, furthermore, almost unavoidable that such encounters bring forth negative memories of the meeting as well as negative memories of the type of leadership provided by such a superior. And all these less-than-joyful encounters stem precisely from a superior's inability or unwillingness to distinguish between simple authority and actual leadership.

Much like the issue of management, authority, whether it is implicit or explicit, is most certainly a partial requirement for leadership, but it is neither the sole nor even the primary requisite of leadership. Authority is but one part of the leadership puzzle, and if it is allowed total dominion over all the other pieces, it degenerates into a simple type of overbearing power that is at first resented by a leader's subordinates, then ignored, and then actively resisted if necessary. And thus, simple authority is not leadership in any meaningful sense.

The manner in which authority, if it is taken to be the primary element of leadership, can be abused is twofold: explicitly and implicitly. Explicitly, it can be used by the individual in the command position to visibly force submission from all other group members to his own will, thus stifling group creativity, motivation, and morale. Implicitly, if the authority invested in a certain position rests solely and primarily in the hands of an individual who is timid or incapable of commanding, then the group suffers because its decision-making capabilities, its problem-solving abilities, and its goal-seeking drive are paralyzed due to a lack of authoritative command and control. It is, therefore, in these two manners that a leader's authority can be abused and thus weaken the leadership presented by any leader to the point of overall ineffectiveness or futility. So these two concerns surrounding the idea of authority and its abuse must always be kept in mind, and actively countered, by any individual who holds a position of leadership.

A further method that can be used to recognize the abuse of authority and to understand the consequences of such abuse is to realize that while leadership fosters obedience due to respect and deference, authority creates obedience out of fear and apprehension. During my military career, this fact was constantly evident, as I knew many soldiers who obeyed their superiors purely out of fear. This fear was generated from the superior's positional clout, which was often unnecessarily flaunted, as well as from the superior's ability to invoke various punishments, a leadership right that was often overused and abused. Such soldiers were not being led; they were simply being commanded and ordered about. This situation eventually caused these soldiers to seek out any means to subvert their superiors, and they would watch and wait for any opportunity to do so. Not only this, but the soldiers would simultaneously seek out a *real* leader within their ranks. Such a leader may not have had explicit authority within the military group, but he gained an implicit authority from the soldiers themselves as they began to place more and more of their trust in this unofficial leader, rather than in the leader that was officially in command.

Furthermore, the creation and continuation of these issues and problems concerning the abuse of authority meant that the military officer trying desperately and overbearingly to assert his authority would slowly lose control of his very group, and would thus lose any chance of making significant gains towards any potential leadership goal that he may have had planned. Such a vicious circle would continue until the entire military unit became ineffective and the military officer's authority ultimately became inconsequential. These examples, furthermore, are obviously not limited to the military environment, but occur in all types of organizations and groups, and thus all types of organizations and groups must guard against any potential abuse of authority.

Authority, therefore, whether it be explicit or implicit, must necessarily be a part of any leader's tool-box, but it must never take up so much space as to dwarf every other element required for a leader to be effective. Indeed, possessing authority does not automatically bestow leadership, but being a leader naturally bestows a type of inherent authority. True leadership, therefore, is always more effective than a simple authoritarian leadership, and this fact should not be forgotten.

Leadership

While it has been explained that both pure management and pure authority, though necessarily a part of leadership, are not the primary elements of leadership—thus having addressed and determined what leadership is *not*—it is still essential to determine what leadership actually *is*. And to do so, it is best to lay out a clear definition of leadership itself.

CATHOLIC LEADERSHIP

Now it cannot be denied that many different definitions of leadership exist, and though it may be a cliché, it is not a stretch to say that there likely exists a different definition of leadership for every single leader. Indeed, consider the following definitions of leadership, all of which grasp some key truth about leadership itself, and overlap with each other, but all of which are ultimately different and varied in their focus and flavor:

- Leadership is the art of influencing and directing people in such a way that will win their obedience, confidence, respect and loyal cooperation in achieving common objectives. – *U. S. Air Force*
- Leadership is influence—nothing more, nothing less. – *John C. Maxwell*
- If your actions inspire others to dream more, learn more, do more and become more, you are a leader. – *John Quincy Adams*
- Leadership is the ability of a superior to influence the behavior of a subordinate or group and persuade them to follow a particular course of action. – *Chester Bernard*
- My definition of a leader…is a man who can persuade people to do what they don't want to do, or do what they're too lazy to do, and like it. – *Harry S. Truman*
- Leadership occurs when one person induces others to work toward some predetermined objectives. – *Joseph L. Massie*
- Leadership is action, not position. – *Donald H. McGannon*
- Leadership can be thought of as a capacity to define oneself to others in a way that clarifies and expands a vision of the future. –*Edwin H. Friedman*
- Leadership is understanding people and involving them to help you do a job. That takes all of the good

characteristics, like integrity, dedication of purpose, selflessness, knowledge, skill, implacability, as well as determination not to accept failure. – *Admiral Arleigh A. Burke*

- The first responsibility of a leader is to define reality. The last is to say thank you. In between the two, the leader must become a servant and a debtor. That sums up the progress of an artful leader. – *Max DePree*
- Management is doing things right; leadership is doing right things. – *Peter F. Drucker*
- Leadership is the art of getting someone else to do something you want done because he wants to do it. – *Dwight Eisenhower*
- Leadership is a function of knowing yourself, having a vision that is well communicated, building trust among colleagues, and taking effective action to realize your own leadership potential. – *Warren Bennis*

All these different leadership definitions have merit—they would not have been mentioned otherwise—and they all provide a good primer to aid us in understanding the key elements behind the concept and definition of leadership. However, in this particular book, what we are interested in is not a definition of leadership in the general sense, but rather, a definition of *Catholic* leadership. And to comprehensively create such a specific and precise definition, we will need to generate a description of leadership that has not been seen before.

So what is Catholic leadership and how should it be defined? First of all, it must of course be in line with the teachings of the Church. It should also be a comprehensive and "tight" definition, while simultaneously providing enough depth to appropriately honor the twin ideas of leadership and Catholicism. And it should be self-sustaining, meaning that even if all that a Catholic leader had in his possession was this bare definition of leadership, without further elaboration or elucidation, then that leader would still gain a powerful insight into what Catholic leadership is and should be. Therefore, with all this in mind, it is judged both appropriate and proper to define Catholic leadership as follows:

In keeping with the example of Christ, the teachings of the Catholic Church and absolute obedience to moral truth, Catholic leadership is both the art and the science of guiding, shepherding, and managing other free-willed persons towards created and sustained goals, aims, and an overall Catholic vision, without solely or explicitly relying on visible authority or coercive power—God willing.

Now, the first portion of this definition should not raise any eyebrows nor be disputed by any faithful Catholic. By necessity, a Catholic cannot be Catholic without practicing what Christ preached, or without clinging to the teachings of the Church, or without holding to the tenets of objective moral truth. Furthermore, holding to these three elements will assist any and every leader in maintaining an overall style of leadership that is moral, good, and true. They will also assist the leader in seeking out and choosing worthy and honorable aims that may not have been chosen without the guiding wisdom embedded in these three elements. It can thus be said, without a shadow of a doubt, that the reason these three factors have been placed at the beginning of our leadership definition is precisely because they are the very things that we must start with before *any* Catholic leading can even take place. They are the first and the unavoidable step. So to be a

Catholic leader, one must start by being truly and honestly Catholic.

Leadership is both an art and a science, and though such an idea may seem strange—for how can leadership be a science?—it is true. Leadership is a science precisely because, much like the practice of science in general, by meticulously and rigorously following and applying the specific leadership techniques and principles that will be provided in this book, any individual will hold the tools necessary to become a strong and effective leader. Any individual will, furthermore, be able to observe his success as well as recreate and reproduce that success to a greater or lesser extent in all experimental leadership situations. And thus, having observation, reproducibility, experimentation as well as firm leadership techniques to experiment with, we have all the necessary criteria to see how leadership can be viewed as a type of science. Yet leadership is also an art form because it requires an artistic touch, making it greatly dependent upon intuition and emotion in order to know *when* and *where* to apply the scientific leadership techniques and principles already spoken of. It simultaneously requires even more artistic flavor in order to know what *amount* of each leadership principle to use in a given leadership situation. Therefore, we reach the inescapable conclusion that to be a leader is to be not only a scientist who is rigorous, repetitious, and consistent in his application of the leadership principles, but also to be an artist who feels which leadership principles should have priority in a specific situation, and how much emphasis should be given to each of these prioritized leadership principles in that same specific situation. Thus, every individual who wishes to be a leader must ensure that he cultivates the traits necessary to develop a precise and exacting scientific mindset, while tempering those traits with the creative and artistic aspects of his personality.

CATHOLIC LEADERSHIP

Guiding. Shepherding. Managing. Each one of these words has been specifically chosen to form the third component of our definition of Catholic leadership, for each of them represents a different aspect of leading. Each one also possesses a unique leadership focus and focal point. To guide entails a frontal-type of leadership. It means providing specific direction and forceful commands to those individuals that the leader is guiding, while simultaneously leading them from the front of the pack without fear or hesitation. It is, in essence, the leadership of an A-Type personality; it is the leadership of the alpha male in a wolf-pack. Or, in a more Catholic sense, it is the leadership of the most holy saints and the unwavering martyrs.

Shepherding, by contrast, naturally brings forth an image of corralling, controlling, and driving forward a large number of generally self-motivated individuals, and this is indeed precisely what shepherding is. A leader shepherds his flock when he knows and trusts his sheep to be energetic and self-motivated, but understands that they still need that energy and motivation focused in a specific direction. Rather than *pulling* his group towards the direction that he wishes to go in—as he does when he guides his group by leading them from the front—the shepherding leader *pushes* his group forward, making necessary corrections and adjustments to their course of direction, but mostly allowing them to move forward under their own steam. Indeed, just as a flock of sheep will, under their own motivation and effort, willingly run and move from danger, the shepherd and his sheep-dog are still required to control and contain where those same self-motivated sheep run, thus corralling and shepherding them in a specific direction. And whereas leading via the guiding method is generally more appropriate for newer and less experienced groups, the shepherding approach is meant for precisely the opposite; it is meant to be used as a leadership style for those groups that are already experienced, knowledgeable, capable, motivated, and driven, but that still require some direction from their leader.

Finally, we arrive at the idea of managing. Now, as we have already spoken about this issue at length, the previously established points concerning management will not be reiterated save to restate the single fact that management is the process of maintaining and enforcing an *already* established goal, direction, or rule. Therefore, when this fact is fully appreciated, it becomes utterly apparent that not only is managing an integral part of effective leadership in general, it is absolutely critical to Catholic leadership specifically. Why? Because in the ultimate sense, the Catholic has always been, currently is, and will always be but a simple manager to the leadership and truth of Jesus Christ. It is undeniable that the entire Catholic Church, though certainly a leader in this world, was ultimately established to manage and maintain the truth and leadership revealed by Christ Himself. And thus, as counter-intuitive as it may seem, in a very real sense the Catholic leader is first and foremost a manager to the goals and aims established by Christ, which is precisely why the first portion of our definition was both so important and so primary.

Moving to the fourth element within our definition of Catholic leadership, we encounter two ideas: the concept of leading free-willed persons as well as the idea of the creation and sustainment of goals, aims, and an overall Catholic vision. We shall deal with the latter issue first. To be a leader is to necessarily create attainable goals as well as set realistic aims for the group you are leading. Such goals can range from the straightforward and short-termed, such as simply deciding what decorations to place in a church for upcoming Christmas celebrations, or to the vastly complex and long-termed, such as building and managing the very same church over its entire lifetime. Furthermore, the goals or aims that are established can be highly specific and detailed, as would be appropriate for the guiding style of leadership, or can be more general and broad, which is more suitable for the shepherding leader. Yet whatever form such goals or aims take, they *must* be made, for without a goal or aim, any group is lost, wandering aimlessly from task to task without overarching focus or direction, thus rendering their work ineffective, uncoordinated, and disjointed. This fact also provides the precise reason why, in addition to just setting goals or aims, the Catholic leader must simultaneously provide an overall Catholic vision for his team, a vision that serves as the root from which all the other goals and aims grow. The leader's vision is his anchor. It is what provides him, as a leader, with the guidance that *he* needs to generate future goals and aims. An overall vision is a thing that stands firm and resolute, even as subordinate goals and aims shift and change. A vision is static while goals and aims are more dynamic. And therefore, to continue with the church analogy for another moment, we can understand that while a leader's overarching vision may be to create, say, the most orthodox, faithful, and popular parish in his region, his subordinate goals and aims will grow from this one firm and stable idea, and will include such things as efficiently and effectively establishing and building a parish, hiring the right people to maintain the overall vision, and managing the parish in line with this same vision. So it is the vision which, though established by the leader himself, also guides the leader in his selection of various goals and aims. Any Catholic leader must, therefore, possess an overall vision for what he wishes to accomplish before setting out other goals or aims.

This idea of setting goals and aims, however, ties into the knowledge that those members of our group for whom we are setting these goals and aims are free-willed, choice-making individuals. And this fact raises two further concerns. The first is that as free persons, any of the team members that we lead are morally free individuals who are open to reject and counter any morally questionable or evil command issued to them by *any* leader, and they would of course be right to do so. Now, this point should not be a concern for the Catholic leader who maintains his Catholicism seriously, as this would indeed prevent him from commanding evil, but it is still an issue to be noted, for even the best leaders falter and should thus not be surprised or resentful to find their subordinates opposing them in these times of moral weakness and failure. But even more importantly, in your leading of such free-willed persons, it is vital to remember that because they are indeed free-willed, your subordinates are ultimately free to either support or reject your vision as well as the leadership that you provide them. And this fact is critical to the leader who is seeking to guide or shepherd free individuals towards a goal that he has established. Just as free-willed individuals who personally choose to follow a specific goal are more motivated and driven to see that goal fulfilled by virtue of their self-chosen adherence to it, so too are free-willed individuals less likely to be motivated and driven towards a goal that they reject. This means that every leader needs to remember that he must not only establish a goal, but he must sell and promote this goal to those that he seeks to lead. Without creating a desire in people to freely follow the goals and aims that we wish them to follow, we will either have no people to lead or we will be leading the resentful and unmotivated. So a vital part of being a leader is generating a yearning for the same goal that you have in those individuals that you wish to lead. And thus all these elements are inseparable from the knowledge that the only individuals that we can lead are *free* individuals, whose freedom, it must be noted, was originally given and granted by God Himself, and this fact should be sufficient to inform us of freedom's importance and centrality to the human condition.

Much like the issue of management, the last major portion of our definition elaborates and expands upon a topic that we have already covered: authority. This part of the definition comes from the apprehension that should exist in all leaders concerning the idea of blatant authority and its use within the leadership structure. While it has already been explained that authority itself is not the issue here, but rather a sole reliance on authority in place of actual leadership, it is this precise point that is expressed in this section of our definition. In the overall context of our characterization of Catholic leadership, we can see that if a leader relies totally on his authority to animate his followers, then he is not so much guiding or shepherding them as he is escorting them, much like prisoners are forcibly escorted by a guard. Now, it is true that the explicit, overt, and clear application of a leader's authority, to be followed without discussion or hesitation, is necessary in certain rare situations, and our definition of Catholic leadership most certainly does not rule out this necessity, but it does restrict such action to only the most exigent of circumstances. This, in turn, ensures that the authority that a leader possesses does not become either a crutch compensating for poor leadership or is rendered limp from overuse. Thus, to be an effective Catholic leader, you must have authority, but you must simultaneously limit its forceful use to only the direst of situations if your aim is to develop and maintain a successful style of leadership.

God willing; this is the final portion of our definition. It is meant to remind us, as Catholic leaders, that ultimately all things are in God's hands. It is meant to reinforce the fact that all our leadership efforts unavoidably rest in God and His providence. And it is meant to make clear that our vision, and our goals, and our aims must be in accordance with the will of God, or else they lose their worth. So this closing element of our definition of Catholic leadership ties every other aspect together and puts those other aspects in their rightful place: behind, and subject to, the will of God.

Now, having explored, explained and understood all these different facets of what we take Catholic leadership to be, a most important question still needs to be asked: Do we see these aspects of leadership reflected in the life and ministry of Jesus Christ? For if we do not, then the very foundation of our leadership, Christ Himself, is separated from the definition of leadership that we are working with, and such a separation is not only undesirable, but is actually untenable.

Fortunately, everything that has so far been discussed and articulated is precisely reflected in the life of Christ. In Christ, we see the perfection of both the natural moral law and truth itself. In Christ and His interactions, as recorded in the Gospels, we see both the scientific use of clear and direct leadership principles—as will be shown throughout this book—as well as the artistic application of these principles to suit various situations and circumstances. In Christ, we see a leader who both guides His flock and shepherds it, but also manages the ultimate vision and plan of redemption established by God the Father, in order to ensure that vision's fulfilment. We also see Christ create different goals and aims, all linked back to His ultimate vision of repentance and redemption. These were goals and aims towards which Christ was unceasingly moving, and through which He drew together

His followers, forming capable disciples who always had their freedom respected, even to the point of Christ *asking* them whether they wished to leave Him of their own free will. In Christ we also see a divine authority demonstrated through His divine miracles, but never such a demonstration of authority as to quash all resistance and freedom from either His followers or His detractors, thus never letting His authority or power override His actual leadership. And finally, in Christ, we see a full, complete, and utter submission to the will of God. Indeed, in all the elements comprising our definition of Catholic leadership, Christ is our exemplar and example. In a very real way, the definition of Catholic leadership does not fit *into* Christ's life, but actually flows and stems *from* it. Our definition comes from Christ; Christ *is* the living definition of Catholic leadership.

With this most important matter now settled, it is possible to put to rest the issue of defining Catholic leadership, and move on to the reason that we should be emulating the particular leader that is Jesus Christ.

CHAPTER 2
FOLLOWING A CARPENTER?

"I MAKE MYSELF a leper with the lepers to gain all for Jesus Christ." These were the words of Father Damien—my middle namesake—written to his brother just after he had volunteered to go live with and minister to a colony of lepers. He was willing to risk not only certain death, but also immense hardship, suffering, and pain for the sake and followership of Christ. In Father Damien's eyes, his own life was at its full worth only if it served as a reflection of the life of Christ Jesus. Imagine willfully going to live with a colony of lepers! In our self-serving society, most people today would not even consider donating money to aid someone with leprosy, let alone going to live amongst them.

In much the same way as with Father Damien, when Father Kolbe voluntarily chose to switch places with a condemned prisoner in the bowels of the Auschwitz Concentration Camp, he did so with Christ on his lips. As he endured weeks of torture, starvation, and dehydration, cramped in a four-by-four concrete cell with nine other men, Father Kolbe was calm and joyful, being a light in the evil darkness that surrounded him. Even before his physical and spiritual trial, Kolbe was remembered by others for sharing his meager food, comforting others with his kind words, and remaining a loving human being amongst the other humans who had been twisted into brutal animals. Thus Father Kolbe's life was also seen by himself to be at its full worth only if it served as a reflection of the life and ministry of Christ. And so it was with countless other martyrs, saints, and missionaries, all of whom have either suffered or died for their commitment to Christ. Even for myself, my life was totally and utterly changed upon my commitment to truly follow Christ and His Church. What I did. What I said. How I acted. What my priorities were. All these things were radically shifted once I placed myself in the ranks behind Christ the leader and began to follow Him faithfully. No doubt the same is true for you as well. In fact, the very reason that I, at the beginning of this chapter, chose to briefly elaborate on the martyrdoms of the two specific priests that I did—and they are now saints, it should be added—as opposed to more famous but dated martyrs, is precisely to show that such transformed soldiers of Christ have not only existed in the far past, but still exist today, right alongside you and me. Indeed, there were more followers of the Lord Jesus Christ martyred in the twentieth century than at any other time in human history.

You, I, Father Damien, Father Kolbe and all those that willingly chose to be shepherded by Christ on this earth, even through fire and death, show us that we are dealing with a leader who has inspired, is inspiring, and will continue to inspire a devotion that is unparalleled in human history. It is truly jaw-dropping to contemplate. The man Jesus, a carpenter from a small town nestled in an insignificant part of the world, and with mostly fishermen and illiterates as His initial followers, would become the most successful and influential leader in human history. When understood in this way, there is something almost miraculous about the whole idea—which of course there actually is! Truly, how else could such a man do the following: radically affect over two thousand years of human history, possess over two billion followers (and counting), inspire countless theologians, engage the deepest philosophers, have the greatest architecture in the world build to glorify Him, generate the most beautiful music and artwork in praise of Him, motivate scientists and scholars, have enough books written about Him to fill ten thousand of the largest libraries, arouse the passions of endless martyrs and saints to love their fellow man and to love Christ Himself, and finally, to have the very calendar that we use based on the time before His birth and then after it. Even these points, as vast as they may be, do not begin to cover all the effects, changes, and alterations that Christ has caused, and has inspired His followers to cause, in this world. And perhaps the greatest of these world-changing elements was the creation and establishment of His Church: the one Holy and Apostolic Catholic Church.

The Catholic Church, its arms spread so far as to touch every portion of the earth, is the oldest and one of the largest institutions to grace the face of the planet. Let that fact sink in for a moment. The Church, which Christ claimed would never have the Gates of Hell prevail against it, has outlasted the reign of kings, emperors, dictators, heretics, pagans, and has even stood firm during the rise and fall of entire civilizations. When all else was failing, it has persevered. It has survived against military attacks, physical attacks, spiritual attacks, intellectual attacks, historical attacks, philosophical attacks, and even internal attacks, outlasting them all and standing like a bulwark that no one has shattered. And during these times, not only has the Church survived, it has thrived. Now, these points cannot be overstated nor overemphasized, not because the glory of the Church should be flaunted, but because all those countless kings, emperors, and dictators were happy to predict the destruction and collapse of the Church under their reign, only to see themselves buried by the very Church they claimed would be the one to die. Indeed, the Church has provided the necessary leadership to overcome any challenge or calamity, and this fact should not be lost on those seeking out an example of leadership to emulate and explore.

Not only is this aspect of survival over all adversity unique, but so is the fact that the Church is vastly larger than the majority of businesses, and yet it thrives. It is more varied than most governmental organizations, and yet it survives. It requires more management due to its far reaching nature than any other international charity, and yet it is vitally effective in its role as shepherd of the faithful. And it possesses the leadership responsibilities for one of the largest cohesive groups of people on earth, and yet it does not falter or wholly collapse under this weight.

It is, therefore, for all these reasons and many others that both Jesus Christ and the Church He founded should be viewed as outstanding examples of leadership. Indeed, if we *minimally* define general leadership as the task of leading other people towards some aim or goal—as has been done as part of the overall definition of Catholic leadership—then Jesus Christ truly is the most influential leader in all of human history. This fact becomes even more significant when it is understood that Jesus, in the human realm, had no official authority or social power, so His leadership ability and influence is that much more surprising and miraculous. Furthermore, the additional fact that the small and insignificant movement created by Jesus and His disciples became the largest and most lasting institution in the world is yet another testament to the power of their leadership. Even non-Catholics should see the great benefit of studying the leadership underpinning the Catholic Church. And non-Christians should see the immense benefit of studying the leadership of Jesus Christ. Indeed, whether or not an individual subscribes to Christianity in general or Catholicism in particular, the durability, scope, and influence of the Catholic Church as well as the founder behind this Church means that they both possess an ability to lead that cannot be denied or ignored. So this timeless example of leadership should be studied and applied by all who would call themselves leaders. And this is precisely what we are going to do.

CHAPTER 3
BUT JESUS AND THE MILITARY?

WHILE THE MAIN topics that were discussed in the two previous chapters—the issue of clearly determining what Catholic leadership actually is, and why Jesus Christ is such an outstanding leader to model ourselves after—most certainly needed to be covered in order to establish a common base from which we could all work, those two former ideas are ultimately unlikely to raise too much general controversy as specific subjects of discussion. Such a willing acceptance, however, will most likely not be as easily forthcoming concerning the next topic under discussion, and the one that is undoubtedly on your mind: How can anyone even dare to suggest that the peaceful and loving Jesus Christ would have anything to do with men steeped in the Profession of Arms? How can the life and the teachings of Jesus be in any way connected to the military, and thus to violence, bloodshed, and warfare? And how can Christ's example of leadership honestly and faithfully have anything to do with the leadership needed by a military officer; conversely, how could a military officer's experiences and trials correlate with those of Christ?

While this connection may, at least at first glance, seem distinctly odd and tentative, it is, in fact, not. Indeed, by the end of this chapter, not only will it be clear how the life of Jesus Christ can relate to the military, it will also be plainly evident that the style of leadership that Jesus embodied is actually more in tune with a military mindset and a soldier's needs than with that of any civilian leader, government official, or corporate executive. As such, Christ's overall life and ministry truly convey an example of leadership that is intimately connected to the Profession of Arms. Furthermore, based on this latter fact, it is also the case that the leadership developed by those persons engaged in the Profession of Arms is simultaneously applicable to the religious and spiritual realms. And ultimately, this cross-related and intimate connection between Christ and society's guardians and protectors can be extracted from two complimentary Christian sources: Sacred Scripture and Church Teachings.

The profession of arms and sacred scripture

The first step to establishing a connection between these two seemingly divergent fields is to determine if there is *any* similarity that can be grasped onto from the sources of Sacred Scripture. Luckily, this is not difficult to do, for even in the Gospels the use of armies is spoken of by Jesus Himself: "My kingdom is not of this world. If my kingdom were of this world, *my servants would have been fighting*, that I might not be delivered over to the Jews. But my kingdom is not from this world" (John 18:36, ESV, emphasis added).

Also from the Gospel of Matthew: "Do you think that I cannot appeal to my Father, and *he will at once send me more than twelve legions of angels?* But how then should the Scriptures be fulfilled, that it must be so?" (Matthew 26:53-54, ESV, emphasis added).

The most interesting and critical aspect to note from these passages is not the fact that they speak of armies of angels, for these types of references can be found throughout the entire Bible, but rather that Jesus Himself is insinuating that if the scriptures did not need to be fulfilled in a precise way—meaning through His own sacrifice—then these angels would certainly be coming to His side and *fighting* in His name! Of course, these verses cannot be readily applied to our present world, as hordes of military angels are not normally seen flying about major metropolitan centers, but nonetheless, the passages do illustrate a distinct connection between a religious ministry and a righteous military. So these initial examples fulfill the purpose of establishing a first link between the two seemingly divergent fields, and thus should weaken the idea that these two areas could never be related.

Moreover, it is also important to note that although Jesus may not have spoken directly about the soldiering profession, when Jesus actually met a soldier—the Roman Centurion—Jesus did not condemn this soldier for his vocation, as would be expected if Jesus was *wholly* against the soldier's profession. Instead, Christ actually told the soldier that his faith was greater than anyone else's in Israel (Luke 7:1-10)! Such a statement can only be viewed as a compliment of the highest order, and should make us think twice about dismissing the idea that the fields of soldiering and Christian spirituality are mutually supporting and cross-related. Furthermore, even though Jesus did not address the issue of human soldiering clearly, the person He considered the greatest living human (Luke 7:24-28), namely John the Baptist, did: "Soldiers also asked him [John the Baptist], 'And we, what shall we do?' And he said to them, 'Do not extort money from anyone by threats or by false accusation, and be content with your wages' " (Luke 3:14, ESV). Like Christ, John the Baptist did not denounce or attack those that questioned him simply because they were soldiers, but instead focused on the specific immorality that might be committed by them from within their chosen vocation. Thus, John the Baptist implicitly warns the soldiers that the inherent danger towards immorality stemmed not from the military profession itself, but rather from how they acted while soldiering, meaning that soldiering itself was not intrinsically evil. And this is not the only example that can be brought forth, for when our focus is returned to Jesus, it is possible to see that while He may not have clearly articulated any specific teachings about using physical force, His own actions provide ample instruction to us concerning this matter.

It is likely obvious to any reader of the Gospels that the message of Jesus Christ is one that hinges on love, peace, and kindness. It is also, however, vital to note that Jesus was not against the judicious application of physical force in order to right a wrong, nor was He an absolute pacifist in any sense. The following story illustrates this fact well:

> The Passover was at hand, and Jesus went up to Jerusalem. In the temple he found those who were selling oxen and sheep and pigeons, and the money-changers sitting there. *And making a whip of cords, he drove them all out of the temple, with the sheep and the oxen.* And he poured out the coins of the money-changers and overturned their tables. And he told those who sold the pigeons, "Take these things away; do not make my Father's house a house of trade" (John 2:13-16, ESV, emphasis added).

And:

> And Jesus entered the temple and drove out all who sold and bought in the temple, and he overturned the tables of the money-changers and the seats of those who sold pigeons. He said to them, "It is written, 'My house shall be called a house of prayer,' but you make it a den of robbers." *And the blind and the lame came to him in*

the temple, and he healed them (Matthew 21:12-14, ESV, emphasis added).

From these two simple passages, the depth of implied instruction that can be drawn forth concerning the use of force is unbelievable. Indeed, as incredible as it may sound, many of the tactics used by Jesus in this incident form the foundation of conduct for modern military forces, as these tactics contain the seeds from which Catholic Just War theory was developed. For example, just as Christ distinctly targets only the merchants in the temple, so too do modern armies use all their resources to distinguish between enemy combatants and non-combatant personnel, often allowing key enemy targets to escape if the potential for non-combat casualties is too high. Next, note that Jesus only uses a whip of cords to drive the merchants from the temple, and places most of His effort on overturning tables and scattering animals. In so doing, Christ demonstrates the ideas of only engaging in activities wholly necessary to the military effort as well as only applying the minimum amount of force required achieve your aim. These facts are especially pertinent when it is considered that Jesus could have used any number of powers, such as raining fire down from heaven, in order to achieve His aim, yet He specifically chose to use the one method that would employ the least amount of force in achieving His necessary goal of driving out the money-changers and merchants. These are indeed two combat principles that all modern soldiers strive for, and that they are concurrently ordered to follow in all circumstances. Finally, Jesus exemplifies the idea of proportionality of force, for once the merchants are out of the temple, Jesus no longer pursues them nor does He seek them out to punish them further. Once He achieves His goal of making them depart the sacred area to conduct their business elsewhere, Jesus immediately returns to preaching, healing, and teaching those around Him. Christ harbors no desire for further retribution, revenge, or retaliation. In much the same way, all military combatants are taught to achieve their mission, but that once that mission is complete then they are to cease all violence and harm. Nor can they ever seek out revenge or retribution once hostilities have ceased.

Linking all these previous points together with Christ's stern warning against being an initial instigator of any unjust violence (Matthew 26:51-52), it is thus possible to see that the core principles of conduct developed from Just War theory are distinctly present even in just these two passages of Sacred Scripture. Consequently, from these short passages, the lessons that Jesus teaches those of us who must make use of physical force in our professional lives—such as soldiers, police officers, or others—are profound. You simply have to look below the surface of the text and draw these lessons out. In so doing, you will see that the military mindset is dependent upon and related directly to Christ Himself. This fact is an unavoidable reality conveyed by Sacred Scripture.

The use of force and church teachings
While we may have had to dig through the Sacred Scriptures in order to draw out the connection between the military life and the life of Jesus Christ, as well as having to dig through those same Scriptures in order to discover the permissibility for the Christian to engage in the combat vocations, the fact of the matter is that these two ideas are easily, clearly, and directly seen in the teachings of the Catholic Church. Indeed, the Profession of Arms is seen as both moral and necessary by the Church. For example, from the *Catechism of the Catholic Church (CCC)*:

Legitimate defense can be not only a right but a grave duty for one who is responsible for the lives of others. The defense of the common good requires that an unjust aggressor be rendered unable to cause harm. For this reason, those who legitimately hold authority also have the right to use arms to repel aggressors against the civil community entrusted to their responsibility (CCC 2265).

And this teaching of the moral responsibility of self-defense and of self-protection extends well beyond those individuals employed as social guardians and protectors; in fact, it actually reaches out and encompasses all people:

Love towards oneself remains a fundamental principle of morality. Therefore it is legitimate to insist on respect for one's own right to life. Someone who defends his life is not guilty of murder even if he is forced to deal his aggressor a lethal blow (CCC 2264).

It is thus clear that the use and employment of violence in the necessary and morally justifiable defense of yourself and others is in no way denied by the Church, which may be a shock to some specific Catholics as well as to other pacifist-leaning Christians. But the use of violence as a justifiable tool in the personal sense is not a sufficient teaching for our purposes, for it is also necessary to determine if a similar teaching extends to the overall use of force and violence in the war-fighting sense, as would be required for military personnel. Yet again however, from the direct teachings of the Church, such violence can indeed be justifiable:

All citizens and all governments are obliged to work for the avoidance of war. However, as long as the danger of war persists and there is no international authority with the necessary competence and power, governments cannot be denied the right of lawful self-defense, once all peace efforts have failed (CCC 2308).

And:

Public authorities...have the right and duty to impose on citizens the obligations necessary for national defense. Those who are sworn to serve their country in the armed forces are servants of the security and freedom of nations. If they carry out their duty honorably, they truly contribute to the common good of the nation and the maintenance of peace (CCC 2310).

So these Church teachings are clear. The necessary and honorable employment of violence, both in a personal and corporate sense, is justifiable under certain circumstances. Yet even with these teachings clearly stated, and even with the acknowledgement that violence may be necessary in specific situations, it must be remembered by all those individuals who would ever have to use such force that, even though it is articulated by the Church as permissible, this does not mean that the moral law is negated during the use of this force (CCC 2312). Nor does it mean that the Catholic can hate those people that he must defend himself against (CCC 2302-2303). Nor does it mean that such violence and warfare should be used without rigorous and thorough consideration and contemplation (CCC 2309). Therefore, regardless of what force can legitimately be used given a warranted circumstance, any Catholic employing such force must always hold fast to the moral law as well as hold true to the love for others that the Church demands.

It should by now be apparent that if the judicious and justified use of violence and force is not only allowed for the Catholic, but is also seen as even moral and noble—as made unambiguous from the combination of Sacred Scripture and Church teachings—then the connection between the Profession of Arms and Catholicism is itself made permissible and warranted. This fact is now beyond dispute. But more importantly, we must also wonder why this connection *should* be made at all, as well as why a comparison between individuals involved in the military vocations and persons of the Faith should even be made in the first place. This is a key issue, and the one that we turn to next.

Linking Jesus and the centurion

While it has been shown that there is indeed a type of connection between Christ's Church—and therefore Christ Himself—and the Profession of Arms, it is through the examination of these two spheres in terms of their level of dedication to a cause that we will ultimately expose the deep similarity between the military mindset and the mindset of a devout Christian believer. This deep similarity will thus explain why we *should* combine Catholicism and the Profession of Arms when it comes to the topic of leadership, as well as why we should then learn from this unique union. So the following passage provides a solid starting point to illuminate this link:

> These twelve Jesus sent out, instructing them, "Heal the sick, raise the dead, cleanse lepers, cast out demons. You received without paying; give without pay. Acquire no gold nor silver nor copper for your belts, no bag for your journey, nor two tunics nor sandals nor a staff, for the laborer deserves his food. And whatever town or village you enter, find out who is worthy in it and stay

there until you depart. Beware of men, for they will deliver you over to courts and flog you in their synagogues, and you will be dragged before governors and kings for my sake, to bear witness before them and the Gentiles...and you will be hated by all for my name's sake. But the one who endures to the end will be saved" (Mathew 10:5, 8-11, 17-19, 22, ESV).

In this passage, we see how every material thing is of secondary importance to Christ and His Apostles. Everything—family, friends, possessions, and money—must be left behind in order for Christ's disciples to fulfill their role as preachers of the Good News. Jesus unmistakably instructs His followers that if they are to act as transmitters of His message, they must place that message above all else. This does not mean that the disciples' family or possessions are forever to be discarded, but rather that they must always stand in second place to the primacy of Jesus Christ and His teachings (Matthew 10:37-38). The Gospels clearly articulate, in various different verses, that Christ's disciples were to be ready to suffer any hardship, deprivation, or abuse in order to achieve their mission of spreading the Good News to all. There could be no avoidance of this requirement; their mission took precedence over all else.

While deployed to Afghanistan, many soldiers experienced the same conditions and deprivations that Christ's disciples had experienced over two thousand years ago (not to mention the hardships that many of Christ's present disciples still experience today). Separated from loved ones, missing wedding anniversaries and children's birthdays, eating hard military rations for weeks on end, and absorbing endless hours of scorching heat or freezing cold, the soldiers suffering through these conditions did so for the same reason that

Christ's disciples did: their mission took precedence over any of their own needs. Many soldiers spent, collectively, over three to four years of their lives deployed away from their families and homes in places such as Afghanistan or Iraq or in the many other warzones that do exist and have existed. They missed seeing their children take their first steps or the birth of their new child, all because they believed in the job that they had volunteered for, and believed that they could bring some good to another part of the world through their sacrifice and suffering. Perhaps the only major difference in the intensity of hardship between such soldiers and the disciples of Jesus was that these soldiers were getting paid for their work while the disciples were not, but even the disciples were allowed to receive free room and board while on the road preaching Christ's Good News! Thus, in terms of the acceptance of suffering and hardship as a necessary prerequisite for the completion of their mission, the lives of volunteer soldiers closely mirror the lives of those that decided to spread the teachings of Jesus Christ.

Now, while serious physical and mental hardships are one way in which to see the connection between those individuals employed in the Profession of Arms and those persons professing the Faith, there is yet another means of establishing this deep connection. Indeed, there is one final, ultimate, and profound similarity between these two areas that still needs articulation, and this final connection grows out of the following passage: "And he [Jesus Christ] said to all, 'If anyone would come after me, let him deny himself and take up his cross daily and follow me. For whoever would save his life will lose it, but *whoever loses his life for my sake* will save it'" (Luke 9:23-24, ESV, emphasis added). To lose one's life for a cause is the ultimate sacrifice, and it is one that soldiers are all too familiar with. It is a gift that can never be returned and is a deed that stands as a final testament of unyielding devotion to a cause. Unlike business leaders or community officials or civil servants, when a military member volunteers for active service, he volunteers his own life, if it be required. For the completion of his mission, the military member must be willing to give *all* that he has. And like soldiers who smother enemy grenades to save their comrades, or firefighters that charge into a burning skyscraper to save a group of trapped civilians, or a police officer that runs towards a gunfight instead of away from it, so too is the Christian believer called to step forward and stand for the Good News, even if doing so might cost him his own life. It is thus this mutual understanding and acceptance of the requirement to place the good of a particular mission over one's own life that binds the Christian believer and the soldier in a manner that is closer than is the case with any other profession. When soldiers freely decide to serve their countries, they are made aware— just as believers are made aware when they choose to follow Jesus—that their earthly lives may be forfeit for a cause greater than themselves. Not only did the disciples accept this reality, they lived it. And even the very sacrifice of Jesus Christ Himself attests to this fact!

So, coming full circle, all these interconnecting points lead us back to the main subject of this book: leadership. If the personal suffering and sacrifice that Jesus asks for from His followers is the same in degree as the suffering and sacrifice that the military asks for from its soldiers, then the leadership techniques that Jesus used to motivate His followers to fulfill His mission can thereby be eminently applied to a military setting. Conversely, the leadership lessons and techniques learned from a military environment can just as readily be used to enhance and strengthen the leadership of any devout Catholic. Whether the focus is on leadership lessons from the life of Jesus Christ or the same types of lessons from a military perspective, the core leadership principles from both these areas are mutually supportive. This is true, in large part, because the core requirement from both fields—placing the success of the mission above all else—is the same in either case. In addition, both the military leader and the Christian leader must not only place the achievement of a particular goal over and above their own needs, but they must also place the good of their followers over and above those same personal needs, just as Christ placed the needs of all humankind before His own. Consequently, these two domains may be separate in their specifics, but they are parallel in their key leadership requirements and aims, so they both need to be learned from if we are to gain the greatest and most comprehensive understanding of leadership that is possible.

Now a worthy objection to this last point that might immediately be raised by the faithful believer is that Christ possessed a few more tools in His tool-box—miracles spring to mind—to inspire His followers than the average military officer, so how can the two still be considered equal in their ability to teach about leadership? But viewing the situation in such a manner once again belies the fact that only a surface examination of the issue has been considered. For while Christ may have been able to perform miracles and heal with the touch of His hands, these healings were only an after-effect of a deeper motivating force that *all* people possess: love. This idea is best summarized by the Apostle Paul:

> If I speak in the tongues of men and of angels, but have not love, I am a noisy gong or a clanging cymbal. And if I have prophetic powers, and understand all mysteries and all knowledge, and if I have all faith, so as to remove mountains, but have not love, I am nothing. If I

give away all I have, and if I deliver up my body to be burned, but have not love, I gain nothing (1 Corinthians 13:1-3, ESV).

It was Jesus' love for the people that drove Him to use His power to aid them, not the opposite, and since such a love is available to all people (at least in theory if not in practice), then the objection at the start of this paragraph does not stand up to scrutiny. Indeed, just as Saint Paul clearly states that any power that lacks the intrinsic qualities of love—such as justice, compassion, or mercy for others—is shallow, the same idea applies to leadership. A modern leader can have all the power or authority that he wants, but if he does not have the leadership that stems from love and faith (as will soon be demonstrated), then he is not a real leader. His followers will fall away from him as soon as the opportunity presents itself. Even Jesus warns His disciples that other individuals will come performing great signs and miracles (Mark 13:21-23), but because they do not possess His deeper message of love for all, then their powers are both empty and heretical. Thus such individuals are to be avoided, because their power will be used for self-aggrandizement rather than the aid of others. And furthermore, such individuals, if they are in secular leadership positions, should indeed be treated in much the same way.

In conclusion, the connection between the life and leadership of Jesus Christ, the lessons of His Church, and the leadership required in military vocations has now been clearly shown to exist in an intimately close and mutually supporting way, both in kind and in degree. Consequently, the idea that the leadership lessons of Jesus Christ could be highly beneficial to a military officer should, at this point, be quite acceptable. In the same vein, the idea that the Christian believer can learn something about leadership from a soldier should also be easily digestible. However, just in case some residual resistance still exists for certain readers concerning this matter, one last Gospel passage, which expresses the inherent leadership connection between a soldier and a believer better than another thousand words ever could, will be provided. For soldiers, it is one of the most often heard scriptural verses, as it is the one that is read by every Christian chaplain on the most solemn of occasions: the passing of a fellow comrade who gave his life for the protection of others, and who, via Christ's own words, thus expresses the greatest level of love possible.

> This is my commandment, that you love one another as I have loved you. Greater love has no one than this, *that someone lays down his life for his friends* (John 15:12-13, ESV, emphasis added).

This *is* what soldiers do. It is the reason that they should be learned from. It is why their leadership ideas should be taken to heart. And these ideas are precisely what will be provided in the rest of this book: the type of ideas concerning leadership that no Catholic should ignore. So read on!

CHAPTER 4
BE A LEADER AND LEAD BY EXAMPLE

WHEN JESUS CALLED on others to take up their cross, He first took up His own. When Jesus called on others to suffer, He originally suffered Himself. When Jesus called on others to forgive, He forgave before any other. When Jesus called on others to obey the Father, He first obeyed the Father unto death. When Jesus called on others to love their neighbors, He loved every one of His neighbors first. When Jesus called on others to strive for perfection, He was perfect. When Jesus called on others to discard hypocrisy, He ensured that none was within Him. When Jesus called on others to pray with humility and honesty, He ensured that He prayed the most humbly and honestly of all. And when Jesus preached, He truly and fully lived the very things that He preached, always leading by His own example.

Now, I did not articulate all of these similar and repetitious statements concerning Jesus Christ—and there could have been many more—simply to be dull and pedantic, but rather to clearly demonstrate that this leader that we are following, namely Jesus Christ, is truly a leader that leads fully and completely by example. His entire life is an example, and this is why He is *the* example to follow in terms of leadership. This is also why we who call ourselves Christians actually do so, for we all strive to live as Christ-like a life as possible. We seek, in essence, to be Christ. Christ is the model for us, not only concerning leadership, but in all things. Such examples as the ones provided demonstrate that Christ truly is a leader worthy of being learned from and emulated. And He is a leader who above all encapsulates the particular leadership principle under discussion. Furthermore, Christ's pattern of always leading by example illustrates the utmost importance of this specific leadership principle, even in comparison to the vitally important leadership principles that are still to be considered. This is why this particular leadership principle is the first one that we must tackle. It may sound blindingly obvious, but to *be* a leader and to lead by *example* are the most important specific things that a leader can do. And though they are separated here for ease of comprehension and articulation, ultimately they are but one leadership principle, for to *be* a leader necessarily entails leading by example. Indeed, if the latter aspect is missing, then the former one will not even exist. Yet what do we mean when we say: lead by example? Or, to be more precise, what is specifically entailed in the idea of leading by example?

Everyone *knows* what leading by example means, yet not everyone *understands* what it entails. Given that this is the most important of leadership principles, the fact that many leaders—as seen in my own experience—do not understand this idea is perhaps a reason for the poor leadership so often demonstrated from those individuals who should know better and from whom more is expected. In essence, to lead by example is to never ask your subordinates to do something that you yourself are not willing to do. It is an ideal that embraces and lives out the mantra: Do as I do, not as I say. At the same time, it wholly and naturally rejects the opposing slogan of: Do as I say, not as I do. In this manner, leading by example is directly linked to the idea of an *involved* leadership. You cannot lead by example if you are not somehow involved in the tasks that you have asked your subordinates to do.

Now a further key point to note is that when I stated that leading by example means being willing to do everything that you ask of your subordinates, the key word in that statement was "willing." The reason that the concept of leading by example requires being *willing* to do what you ask your subordinates to do, rather than actually and directly doing it in every instance, is because of the simple fact that you, as a leader, may ultimately not be able to do everything that you ask of your subordinates. Indeed, you may not be able to do so due to time constraints, or technical constraints, or knowledge constraints, or a host of other legitimate and unavoidable barriers. But regardless of whether you can or cannot, in each specific instance, do the particular thing that you are asking your subordinates to do, what your subordinates need to know from past experience is that you *do* lead by example whenever you *can* do so. Knowing this provides your followers with the very knowledge that you wish them to have: namely, they will know that if you could lead them by personal example, you would do so, because they will have seen from their past experience that you lead by example whenever you can. Essentially, they will thus know that you are always *willing* to lead by example, even if you cannot do so in every particular instance.

To understand this concept better, consider the following example from my military past. Many days, my platoon and I would start work with an intensive fitness-training session. During a number of these sessions, due to other necessary commitments, I would be unable to attend the physical training and was thus unable to lead my platoon via my own personal example in those instances. However, because my platoon always knew that if I could have been present at the training sessions, I would have been, and because they knew that even on my own time I worked out quite vigorously to make up for any platoon sessions that I missed, every member of my platoon still saw me as leading them by example, even though at times I was obviously not physically present to do so. Thus, the knowledge that I was always willing to do whatever I asked my platoon to do was the key that transformed me into a leader who was, in the eyes of my men, known to always lead by example.

Now, the method used to develop this knowledge stems from one rule: As a leader, seek to physically and personally lead by example in every available instance, manner, location, and situation, no matter how significant or insignificant the circumstances may be. So if I ask my subordinates to provide me with only the highest quality work when they submit it to me, then I better ensure that I am providing them with an even higher quality of work. If I ask my subordinates to make coherent and cohesive presentations, I must ensure that my presentations are as tight, precise, and sharp as any of theirs. If I ask my subordinates to ensure that their appearance is neat and tidy, then I better be the best dressed individual out of all of them. If I ask my subordinates to stay as late as necessary to complete a task that I have assigned them, then I, as their leader, should be the very last one to leave, making sure all my subordinates are comfortably home before I even exit the office. And if I ask my subordinates to march 20 miles in the cold autumn air, with a heavy 80-pound pack on their backs, then I best be willing to do the same march with 80 pounds plus the 10-pound platoon radio, which is something I did indeed do!

So while these illustrations could be multiplied a thousand times over, I ultimately leave it up to you to discover and imagine, given your particular profession, any further pertinent examples. What is in large part very clear, however, is that leading by example is a goal that can be accomplished and demonstrated in all tasks, even ones of the very smallest sort. And it is precisely by leading via your example during such small and seemingly unimportant occasions that your willingness, as a leader, to lead by example in each and every possible instance will be noted and remembered by your subordinates. It is, therefore, through leading by example in these minor tasks, but doing so on a constant basis, that you will generate an aura around you in the eyes of your subordinates, an aura that marks you as a leader who truly leads by example. Your subordinates will never forget this fact, which means that you, as a leader, will have achieved a major success in terms of promoting and reinforcing your leadership strength and authority.

Constantly lead by example in the details, and the rest shall follow, for your men will never forget those very details that you may think are insignificant. Indeed, there is a good reason that the most common leadership slogan that I ever heard during my military training was: Always lead from the front! For to lead from the metaphorical front, and quite often the very literal one, means to always lead by example. To be in front is to be an example, for to be in front signifies that your men are to follow you, and thus to follow your example. So always remind yourself to lead by example, always remember to lead from the front!

Having addressed the issue of leading your team via your own personal example, and thus solidifying this one aspect of leadership, it is now necessary to turn to the idea of *being* a leader. What does this mean? What does it mean to *be* a leader? And what does it mean to *be* a leader in terms of a leadership principle?

The reason that this seemingly obvious idea needs to be articulated and reinforced is that, once again, many so-called leaders forget that to *be* a leader, they must be ready, at all times and in all places, to fulfill the duties of a leader. Too many of such "leaders" are leaders in name only and actually are, in reality, nothing but followers in the garb of a leader. In such cases, the so-called "leader" is even more of a detriment to an organization than any incompetent subordinate, for such a "leader" has a much wider overall affect than any subordinate could ever have. Furthermore, such a "leader" causes all of his subordinates to suffer as a result of his own inabilities. This is why *being* a leader is a leadership principle without which no actual leadership is even possible. And to *be* a leader, you need to understand, acknowledge, and always be prepared to carry out the primary tasks of leading: setting the example, decision making, problem solving, managing, coordinating, and always being at the forefront of any organizational challenge.

We have already discussed the first of these points—leading by example—which is arguably the most important of the group, and which, if done well, will give you some latitude to make mistakes in the other areas. Indeed, subordinates who see that you are a leader who always strives to lead by example, regardless of the situation or circumstance, truly will cut you some slack if you are not the best problem solver or the best manager or so on and so forth. Yet these other elements are still crucial to *being* a leader, and they must therefore be addressed.

A leader makes decisions; there is no way around this fact. As a leader, you will be expected to make decisions that range from the most important, such as setting the overall mission for your entire organizational group, to the most mundane, such as determining the dress code that your subordinates must adhere to. Furthermore, regardless of the situation or the circumstances, as the leader you will be expected to make those decisions; indeed, regardless of how stressful or dangerous the scene, *you* are the decision maker, and your followers will look primarily to you for guidance and direction in such situations. In fact, the more stressful and uncertain the situation, the more your subordinates will look to you for a decision on which course of action to take. I recall an operation in Afghanistan where, upon entering a compound in which we expected to find aggressive enemies and bodyguards, instead we found women and children. And as opposed to finding the two-storey house that we had planned for, we found a house with a totally different lay-out. Now, this may not sound like a significant difference, but when you are entering a compound armed and ready to be engaged, having the plan completely change in an instant is a serious and stressful event. It was precisely in this circumstance, where everything we had previously planned had been thrown out the window, that my soldiers looked to me for immediate and instant decision making in this new situation. And make immediate decisions I did, for I was the leader of my platoon and that was my job.

Remember, furthermore, that if you as a leader make a decision, then your whole team makes a decision, for they follow you. But the opposite is also the case. If you *fail* to make a decision, then your whole team fails at it as well, and the repercussions for such a failure can be most severe. You must, therefore, prepare and train yourself to make decisions, and to make them instantly if necessary. If you have problems with this leadership duty, then start with small daily decisions that you can make consistently and confidently, and this will create the framework for making the larger and more important decisions when the time comes to do so. Additionally, as a leader, do not be afraid to change your mind concerning your decisions if necessary, but also, do not be afraid to be firm in your decisions, as either one of these options may be the best course of action in a given situation.

Also bear in mind that an imperfect but workable decision made on time, is always better than a perfect decision made too late. Finally, note that Christ teaches us these facts as well, for He was the one making the decisions as to where He and His disciples would go, or when His disciples would be sent out to preach, or what His group's next course of action would be. Christ was the decision maker! So as a leader, be prepared to make decisions, for if you do not do so, everyone will suffer.

Closely linked to the idea of decision making, and actually a prerequisite for it, is the skill of problem solving. You cannot make decisions concerning difficult problems without first overcoming them via problem-solving techniques. Now, providing a wide range of different problem-solving methods is beyond the scope or purpose of this leadership principle, and as everyone has certainly solved problems of different varieties in the past, then everyone has some experience in problem solving. Yet two main points concerning problem solving are worthy of mention. The first is to always remember that you are the leader of a *group*, and thus you have a wealth of knowledge and insight within the collective experience of your subordinates that can be extracted and used to overcome a number of different obstacles that you might have trouble overcoming alone. The second point links back to leading by example, and this point is that as the team leader, you are expected to be the main problem solver and set the example in this field for others. So while your subordinates' experience and expertise is immensely valuable, the ultimate problem-solving responsibility still rests on your shoulders. Therefore, you must accept these points and prepare for them.

When we were discussing the definition of Catholic leadership, I mentioned that while leadership is itself not reducible to management, it does include management as one of its necessary components. Management is thus part of *being* a leader and must be discussed. In addition, for our purposes here, it is possible to deal with the idea of management and coordination together, as they are conjoined in significant ways. Now, as a Platoon Commander, I had to be intensely aware of all the strengths and weaknesses of my various subordinates. I also had to be aware of their unique skill sets and technical knowledge. And with this knowledge, I then had to integrate it into the various tasks and objectives that I needed my platoon to achieve within specific timeframes. In this manner, as the platoon's leader, I was also the platoon's coordinator. Knowing the tasks that needed to be accomplished and knowing within what timeframe they needed to be achieved, it was my responsibility to coordinate between the tasks I had, and between the different times in which those tasks needed to be accomplished, and between the type and number of personnel that I had at my disposal as well as between the various material resources needed to fulfill all these tasks. This is indeed a duty that every leader must prepare for, especially since the leader is naturally seen as being the team's chief and primary coordinator. So know your personnel well. Know their skills sets and knowledge. Also know the tasks you must complete and the time that you have to complete them. Finally, know that coordination is a vital component of leadership and management, and as such cannot be avoided or neglected.

In a similar manner to coordination, management requires not only knowing the strengths and weaknesses of your subordinates, but also knowing all the administrative aspects of your organization. You need to know the status of the equipment and stores that you possess and are in control of. You need to be aware of the financial and material situation of your company. You need to have knowledge of all the private issues surrounding your subordinates. Are they currently having any personal problems? Are they having any family issues that are on-going and are affecting their work? Are they under great stress for some reason? Do they have a medical condition? Such concerns are necessary for any manager to know and accurately keep track of. Indeed, imagine running and managing a family household, and now extend all the skills required to do that task out to managing an entire group of people. You must know that group of people as well as you know your own family. And even though this is not a perfect analogy—although it is one that should be quite illuminating for Catholics with the virtuous propensity for large families—it is an analogy that will provide you with a good general idea of the type of management required to be a worthy leader. In fact, I remember that when I led my platoon, it helped me a great deal to quite literally think of myself as my soldiers' father, and this gave me an initial framework that I could use to manage them effectively. So being a precise coordinator and a knowledgeable manager are inescapable components to being a leader.

The last cogent point that pertains to this leadership principle is to always keep in mind that you are nothing more and nothing less than a leader. What this means is that you should not take on the roles and tasks that do not belong within your purview as a leader, as well as meaning that you are to lead your subordinates, *not micro-manage them*. So when you delegate specific tasks to certain appropriate subordinates, then make sure that you do not incessantly look over the shoulder of those same subordinates as they strive to carry out the task assigned to them. Granted, if the subordinate is incompetent or incapable of properly completing the assigned task, then as a leader you must step in and sort out the matter, but such action should be the exception rather than the rule. Within my own platoon, for example, I knew that my Platoon

Signaler was the communications expert within our group, and that it was not my job as the Platoon Commander to fix the radio, but his. So while I may have tasked the Signaler to fix the radio, I would not tell him how to do it, nor would I be overshadowing him or constantly observing him to make sure that he was fixing it properly. Assign the task and then let your people get on with it!

It is interesting to note that we actually do see this aspect of leadership from Jesus. For example, when Christ tasks His disciples to go out and preach to the world, we see Jesus assign His disciples that specific mission, but then leave those same disciples to their own devices; the disciples are allowed to go where they wish and they are allowed to preach in the manner that they desire. Now, Jesus Christ, humorously enough, may be micro-managing His disciples because, as He is God, He ultimately already knows what His disciples are going to do, but Christ is certainly not micro-managing them in any earthly sense, which is the sense that is important to us. Instead, Jesus is delegating the task that He needs accomplished and then allowing His disciples to go out and complete it in their own manner.

Finally, let me confess that in all honesty, I cannot think of one specific military story that accurately, totally, and comprehensively illustrates this leadership principle of *Lead by example and Be a leader*—even though some of the stories already provided do illustrate parts of it. The reason that I cannot provide such a story is that, without exaggeration, every single one of the leadership situations that I encountered required me to fully lead by example and to truly *be* a leader. This was the one leadership principle that was literally beat into me from the very beginning of my military training, and it was the one leadership principle that I thus strictly and wholly applied from the very start of my military career. And this fact should tell you a great deal about this leadership principle's importance. So remember: *Always* lead by example and always *be* a leader! Those counting on you deserve nothing less.

CHAPTER 5
GATHER INTELLIGENCE, STAY CURRENT, REMAIN AWARE

YOU ARE a commander and a chief. You are a decision maker and a goal setter. You are the leader of men and women. You are a Catholic leader! And as a Catholic leader, you will be required, necessarily and unavoidably, to make decisions and choose courses of action that will weigh on your shoulders for a great many years. These decisions will, furthermore, weigh most heavily on the men and women that you lead, for your decisions will affect them in the most intimate and important of ways. For myself, as a military officer, I was indeed always and acutely aware that my decisions—because they could literally cause the death of the subordinates linked to me—were of the most serious and vital sort, influencing every facet of my followers' existence. So for a leader, making good, right, and competent decisions is the most important of activities. The question, therefore, is how do we make such decisions and what tools are necessary and crucial to do so? The first tool that is indispensable to decision making is information, and not just information, but *intelligence*. In terms of leadership, what is intelligence? And what is the difference between intelligence and simple information? It is by first answering the latter question that we can then address the former one.

The word *information* is one that we hear every day in common conversation, and we may even hear the term *intelligence*, although likely not as often. And even though they are both intimately interconnected, there is a crucial difference between these two terms. Essentially, *information* is just that: unfiltered and unprocessed information. It is any type of information that is provided to you. *Intelligence*, by contrast, is assessed information. It is information that has been filtered, processed, and investigated as well as thoroughly and rigorously assessed. This is a difference that cannot be overemphasized. To understand this via an analogy, consider the following: information is like hearing a rumor from someone that you do not know that well and then just taking that rumor at face value, whereas intelligence is like receiving the same rumor, but then investigating the allegation, seeing if anyone else has heard the rumor, trying to get to the source of the rumor, testing the credibility of the rumor spreaders, and attempting to get physical evidence to support the rumor, all the while also rigorously assessing all your new discoveries and determinations concerning the rumor itself. Thus, as stated, intelligence is assessed information, and this is precisely why it is *intelligence* that is crucial to every leader, not just information. Information can be, and often is, false, distorted, and/or misguided, whereas intelligence minimizes these dangers to the greatest degree. And what decision maker can risk making choices based on false, distorted, or misguided information? None can! It is, therefore, the key task of every leader not only to understand that every piece of information received must be transformed into intelligence, but also to act on this knowledge, ensuring that it is applied as often and as comprehensively as possible.

There still exist, however, further factors that need consideration when converting information into intelligence: being current and remaining aware. In the first case, and in order for it to be of the highest quality, intelligence needs to be developed from information that is as current and as up-to-date as possible, for information that is current holds the best chance of being correct, or at least as correct as possible. In military terms, just imagine if you were planning a major combat operation based on intelligence concerning the enemy's disposition and strength that was six months old. Such an act would be obvious lunacy, for the simple fact is that in six months, the enemy could have totally changed his strategic and tactical positioning, as well as increased or decreased his overall strength. As such, any commander who would lead an attack based on such intelligence is a commander who trusts "luck" too much, as his intelligence would be essentially worthless. And this idea is the same for any other field or profession. Business leaders do not make critical decisions based on old or out-dated information. Sports teams do not make decisions on how to play against their rivals based on how those rivals were playing last season. And the Church re-affirms and re-emphasizes key teachings in a manner that is largely based on the current cultural climate that the Church stands firmly within, thus providing the faithful with a way to understand what the Church teaches in light of the culture of the day. So the need to be and stay current with your information-gathering is crucial.

It must be remembered, however, that staying current does not mean being influenced or overcome by the times, or the culture, or the situation that you find yourself in. Instead, it means that you must be current concerning what those times, that culture, and that situation entail and promote, even as you stand against them. Nor does being current mean that historical intelligence is somehow invalid, for this is again not the case at all. Rather, it simply means that historical intelligence—which means intelligence from the past that may be applicable to the current situation, such as intelligence on an enemy's language or culture or historical battle tactics—must be taken from the most up-to-date and current historical sources (granting that the trustworthiness and scholarly rigor of these current sources is equal to earlier sources) in order to ensure that any historical intelligence is as complete as it could possibly be.

The second aspect of converting information into intelligence is to stay aware, and this particular idea also has a number of additional sub-points that arise from it. The first issue is that staying aware means being knowledgeable of the sources from which your information, and thus your future intelligence, is coming from. Being aware of and knowing your sources is critical to the intelligence process, for whether your sources are trustworthy, intelligent, perceptive, objective, discerning, and capable will tell you a great deal about how to take and assess the information that they provide you with. Knowing, for example, an individual's, or a newspaper's, or a news source's biases will dictate, to a great extent, the manner in which you take the information provided by these sources. Everyone has seen such examples before, because everyone has been exposed to biased individuals or biased news sources before, and thus everyone knows how they have taken the information provided by such sources: with a very large pinch of salt! Furthermore, from a Catholic perspective, it is also endlessly possible to see how, in recent years, secular information sources demonstrate their biases and poor provision of objective information concerning Catholic teachings and cultural issues. And therefore, it is possible to see how, for the Catholic leader, being aware of your sources is utterly crucial to extracting proper intelligence from the poor information that such sources provide.

The second point arising from the idea of being aware is that as a leader, you must not only be aware of the sources that you have, you must also be aware of sources *in general*. What this means is that you must always be aware of new places and new means by which to gain the latest information that can thus be transformed into up-to-the-minute intelligence. The internet, for example, is a beautiful instance of "being aware" in action; many years ago the internet became a new and outstanding means of gathering information, a fact that would have been lost on any leader that did not pay attention to it and was thus not aware of its information-gathering potential. So a leader must always be attentive and alert to the arrival, growth, and development of new sources of information.

Directly linked to this second point is what could be seen as point two-and-a-half, for while it is not significant enough to be a self-standing factor, it is worthy of mention nonetheless. This sub-point stems from the fact that in addition to being aware of new sources of information, we must simultaneously be aware of when information sources need to be dropped. It is necessary to know when certain sources of possible information have become so biased, jaded, and unworthy that they should be dropped as sources. To come back to our internet example, it is common knowledge that there are certain specific writers and/or certain specific websites that are so clearly biased and so clearly focused in one direction only—to the detriment of any serious objectivity—that they are not even worthy of being read. And this internet example can obviously be extended to various other information providers. Consequently, it is a leadership requirement to be both aware of potentially new sources of information as well as aware of old sources of information that need to be discarded. For it is by properly accomplishing both these tasks that the path towards the best intelligence, and thus the best decisions, is trod.

Having now explained the difference between intelligence and simple information, as well as having explained the need to be as current as possible with the information that you receive, and having addressed the overall requirement to remain aware, we still need to cover one final topic: the Intelligence Process. Though perhaps strange sounding, what this term essentially expresses is the process by which we transform information into intelligence. And this process is composed of four simple and ordered steps: establish the focus, gather relevant information, assess all information, and decide from intelligence.

Since everyone's time, effort, and energy are finite and limited, it is necessary, before taking any action in relation to gathering information, to establish the focus of your time, effort, and energy. Therefore, the first step of the intelligence process is to determine what the intelligence is needed for and what the focus of our information gathering needs to be. This first step thereby assists in narrowing down our center of attention to something more manageable as well as specific enough for detailed information to be gathered concerning it. Without this step, our information-gathering will either be so diffuse as to be worthless, or so demanding as to not leave us time for any other step. Thus, this first step is a necessary and critical aspect of the Intelligence Process.

Having established our focus, we now have to gather all the information that is pertinent to that established focus. This step means collecting information from every available source that is relevant to our situation. Note that this step is *not* where we are concerned with our specific sources or the currency of the information that we are receiving. Rather, at this point, we should only be concerned with the collection and collation of information. Having all this information now gathered and collected, we move to the third step.

Assessing our information is the third step, and it is the one in which all our information is transformed into intelligence. This is where the examination of the collected information occurs. It is here that we check our sources for their currency as well as where we extend our awareness to review the quality, knowledge, and objectivity of the sources from which the information was gathered. This is where we compare all the information gathered in order to determine links between the various pieces of information and to make connections between disparate facts and separate chucks of knowledge. And this is where we assess, appraise, evaluate, analyze, and compile all our separate information into a coherent and comprehensive whole, meaning that we have just generated actual intelligence. Indeed, by the time the third step is complete, we are no longer in possession of information, but rather valuable, precious, and decision-ready intelligence.

Finally, as a leader who has just created intelligence that is geared towards our particular focus, we must now of course decide to act based on this intelligence. If a decision is not made, then the intelligence, and the entire Intelligence Process that has just been described, has been a waste of time and effort. Thus, once that intelligence is in hand, it is necessary to act on it; it is necessary, as a leader, to make an intelligence-based decision and lead the way!

Now this entire Intelligence Process, due to its categorization and separation of parts, may seem odd, but it is actually a process that every single person employs every single day, in almost every single decision that they make. For example, when we plan a trip or a vacation, we all instinctively do the following: first, we establish a focus as to where and when we will take the trip; second, we then collect information about the weather at that location, the activities that we can do, the quality of the location, and so on and so forth; third, we assess that information to see if it can be trusted and if it is more likely true than not; fourth, we ultimately make a decision whether or not to take the trip based on the intelligence that we have generated. So this entire Intelligence Process is really as common and as basic as it could be. This means that, upon reflection, the Intelligence Process should be both easy and simple for you to understand and apply. Indeed, since we all use this process in our daily lives, then as leaders, we can apply it to daily leadership situations without problem or concern. And thus the Intelligence Process should be consciously employed as often as possible, for doing so will significantly improve the decisions of any leader, making the Intelligence Process as valuable as it is needed.

Finally, in reference to the overall leadership principle that is being discussed in this chapter, an additional question remains: Did Jesus Christ practice and demonstrate this leadership principle in His own life? The answer to this latter question is that not only did Jesus demonstrate this principle, but He did so in a Gospel passage that is of the utmost importance to the Catholic believer.

> Now when Jesus came into the district of Caesarea Philippi, he asked his disciples, "Who do people say that the Son of Man is?" And they said, "Some say John the Baptist, others say Elijah, and others Jeremiah or one of the prophets." He said to them, "But who do you say that I am?" Simon Peter replied, "You are the Christ, the Son of the living God." And Jesus answered him, "Blessed are you, Simon Bar-Jonah! For flesh and blood has not revealed this to you, but my Father who is in heaven. And I tell you, you are Peter, and on this rock I will build my church, and the gates of hell shall not prevail against it (Matthew 16:13-18, ESV).

Here are a number of key verses that exemplify the entire leadership principle under discussion as well as the Intelligence Process that was articulated. First, we see Jesus Christ establishing the focus of His inquiry: namely, Christ wishes to know who or what people—both people in general and His disciples in particular—think He is. To that end, Christ focuses His question towards this specific aim. Second, Christ gathers information, asking all His disciples the very question that He is focused on. Third, Christ assesses the information that He has been given, and it is here that we can see Christ's implicit assessment of His information sources, as well as His reception of current and timely information. Furthermore, Christ's assessment of these sources is so good that with Simon Peter, Christ clearly perceives that Simon's answer comes from a source that is beyond Simon Peter himself. So Christ makes the most accurate assessment of the information that He has been given, transforming it into crucial and vital intelligence that both aids Him and informs Him of the current success and status of His earthly preaching mission.

Now, concerning the fourth aspect of the Intelligence Process, where Christ makes a decision based on the intelligence generated, we can turn to the Gospel of Luke, which recounts the same episode, but with an ending that demonstrates this fourth point:

> Now it happened that as he was praying alone, the disciples were with him. And he asked them, "Who do the crowds say that I am?" And they answered, "John the Baptist. But others say, Elijah, and others, that one of the prophets of old has risen." Then he said to them, "But who do you say that I am?" And Peter answered, "The Christ of God."

CATHOLIC LEADERSHIP

And he strictly charged and commanded them to tell this to no one, saying, "The Son of Man must suffer many things and be rejected by the elders and chief priests and scribes, and be killed, and on the third day be raised" (Luke 9:18-22, ESV, emphasis added).

We indeed see the fourth element of the Intelligence Process demonstrated here, for having created the intelligence that He required, Christ acts on this intelligence, deciding to tell His disciples that now that they know this fact about Him—that He is the Christ—they are to tell no one about it. This decision is firm and decisive, based directly on the intelligence that Christ received from His disciples, and it is a decision which, whether followed or not, would have far-reaching repercussions for Christ's earthly mission. So, from the Gospel narratives surrounding Jesus Christ Himself, it is possible to see just how essential this specific leadership principle is.

In my own experience as an Intelligence Officer, I can attest to the necessity and vitality of gathering intelligence, staying current, and remaining aware. For while it is indeed a running military joke that "military intelligence" is an oxymoron (and regardless of the humor that this joke generates), there is truly no competent military commander who would act, in any capacity, without at least some intelligence backing him up. I remember spending countless hours employing the Intelligence Process to produce relevant and comprehensive intelligence for my military commanders to use and make decisions with. Such decisions, based on this intelligence, would involve the lives of many soldiers, as well as a great deal of material, not to mention the possible loss of our tactical and strategic advantage. It is thus easy to understand why the intelligence provided to these commanders would be of the utmost importance. And my experience as a military intelligence officer was at the lower end of the scale, whereas other intelligence officers were providing intelligence to military commanders at the highest level, leading to military operations of the grandest scale. Just imagine, from history, how important the intelligence effort was for such massive military operations as the D-Day landings during World War II. Or, for a more modern example, the invasion of Iraq in 2003—which, in reference to the issue of weapons of mass destruction and their overt absence after the invasion, shows the sheer necessity of timely, accurate, and objective intelligence in the decision-making process. From all these examples and more, it is easy to see the necessity of gathering intelligence, staying current, and remaining aware. Therefore, as a leader, you cannot avoid or neglect this leadership principle if your decision making is to be as accurate, capable, and objective as possible.

CHAPTER 6
BETTER TO GIVE THAN TO RECEIVE

HONEST TO GOD (pun intended), it was so bloody cold that your spit would almost freeze solid the moment that it hit the ground. Your hands and feet were freezing no matter how thick your gloves or your boots were. And the thermometer could not even go any lower. It was cold! Moreover, this is not even mentioning the cutting wind or the blowing snow that would invade your personal space uninvited at the most unwelcome of times, getting through even your thickest layers and chilling you down to your very bones. Regrettably, this was just the kind of weather that had been with me, and by extension with my soldiers, all week, as we were on a military exercise during one of Canada's normal winters. And right in the middle of that exercise, late at night, when even my blood was running cold and my return to a warm bed was far off on the horizon, I remember our Company Quarter Master arriving with hot soup in tow, soup hot enough to burn our insides and even keep us warm for the rest of the night.

Being in a partially administrative bivouac position at the time (meaning that we were not on high alert), and having received permission to do so, our entire company of over one hundred soldiers quickly emerged from their tents and pretty much gathered around the Quarter Master's newly arrived truck. The soup, just pulled out of the back, was already cooling in the freezing weather, even though it was sealed in a special protective container. Everyone knew that the soup would not stay hot for long, and so we all lined up to try to get first "dibs" on a cup of it.

Yet outside this line of quickly formed troops did I and the various other officers stand, shivering in the cold. Though imbued with the rank and the authority to overtake all of the soldiers and obtain the soup first, thus getting the warmest portion, we waited for everyone else to go first. Nor was this in any way surprising or novel to our band of officers, as it was actually military policy that all soldiers, in order from the lowest rank to the highest, eat before any officer did. Indeed, this was a policy that made good sense from a leadership perspective. Yet, with my hands numb from the cold, it was not a policy that I necessarily *liked* at that moment in time. And with over a hundred soldiers to get through, the wait suddenly looked very lengthy.

Finally, after what seemed to be an even longer wait than expected, I was able to stand in line and get a small amount of soup poured into my military tin cup, although by now it was devoid of most of its meatier ingredients. The first sip confirmed my anticipated fear. The soup was cold. Or, to be more precise, it was no longer warm enough to affect my freezing condition in any significant way. The curse that then escaped my lips was as angry as it was unbecoming, but the fact was that I was damn cold, and that small amount of soup, in those conditions, was a prize worth more than gold—truly, it only takes a few such instances of deprivation and suffering to make you endlessly appreciate the little things that so many individuals in our modern world take for granted.

A wave of resentment then swept over me, and I, ever so briefly, felt a burning bitterness for the soldiers that I was supposed to lead, soldiers that I had to take care of before I took care of myself. With this anger now in me, and just as I prepared to pour the remainder of my soup onto the ground out of infantile spite, one of my younger soldiers approached me. Not only did he approach me, but he actually told me that he wanted to give me some of his soup! He said that because he knew mine would be cold since I had had to wait for so long, he wished to give me some of his, which though not substantially warmer than mine, was warm enough. And though I ultimately declined his kind offer, this soldier's few words melted away any lingering resentment that I felt. What a lesson! I thought that I had had the right, or at least the emotional justification, to be bitter and angry at my men, but here were my soldiers willingly trying to care for me at a cost to themselves, just as I had done for them. And it was in this instance, rather earlier on in my military career, that I learned a fundamental leadership lesson that would be reinforced time and time again: it is better to give than to receive, for if you give to your soldiers fully, they will always ensure that you receive exactly what you need.

Now, while this principle seems simple enough, and indeed it is, it is also necessary to understand what precisely can be given. The reason for this explanation is because all too often in our modern culture, we equate giving in general with the giving of material possessions. But the giving of such material things is, in fact, one of the lower forms of giving that a leader can engage in. As a first example, and a most important one, a leader can actually give of his character, integrity, and morals. What this means is that the leader gives to his subordinates by setting the moral example and standard, thus removing the pressure from them to hold to a moral pattern that is in opposition or tension to the leader himself. And in so doing, such giving will undoubtedly lead to a leader's followers providing moral support right back to the leader himself. Second, a leader can give his time, which means that the leader must always use his time for his subordinates before he uses it for his own purposes. By doing so, the leader will ensure that he naturally receives the maximum of his subordinates' time, attention, and effort. In the same way as with these other examples, a leader can also give his knowledge and his patience and his emotion and his concern and his care and his praise and his effort and his energy and his discipline and his love. All these things, and many more, a leader *must* give to those that follow and rely on him. Lastly, a leader can give his subordinates those material items that are required for a given situation. Such material things can range from the most minor form of material item, such as buying a subordinate a cup of coffee, to the most drastic and dramatic form, such as giving your subordinate the last warm cup of coffee during a mind-numbingly cold winter blizzard. Any such acts of giving, whether they are one singular drastic act, or a plethora of minor ones, will all build up over time to provide such a strong impression of your *giving* character—as long as it is genuine—that this impression will be unmistakable to your subordinates. It will also simultaneously increase their faith in you as a valued, caring, and ideal leader.

Understanding that there are so many things, both material and immaterial, that a leader can give to his subordinates, it is easy to see how such *giving* is available to a leader at any time and in any place. Every situation presents an opportunity for a leader to give to his followers. Indeed, even when he has nothing material with him, a leader has the ability to provide his time or his patience or his knowledge or his caring or any number of other things that he always possesses, for these things are *in* him to give. It is, therefore, clear that all temporal situations and circumstances provide every leader with a chance to give to his subordinates in one manner or another. No excuse can thus exist for the neglect of this specific leadership principle. But it also needs to be noted that this principle not only applies to a leader's subordinates, but also to his superiors and his peers. For even though your superiors and peers should be practicing this leadership principle in relation to you, there may arise certain instances where they falter or fail in their own efforts, and this will thus necessitate that you step up and support them in their time of need. To fail to do so would mean that your actual status as a true and honest Catholic leader would be less than sure.

It should also be acknowledged that the methods by which a leader can give to his subordinates can either be covert, overt, or both. Or, to phrase the issue in different terms, a leader can give either directly, indirectly, or both. Now, to use an example that was already mentioned, direct giving would be the equivalent of providing your last cup of warm coffee, already in your hand, directly to a subordinate who is freezing and cold. Indirect giving, by contrast, and to use the same type of example, would be like refraining from taking any coffee in the first place, thus indirectly ensuring that all your subordinates have the opportunity to receive some before you do. So these two methods, or a combination thereof, form the primary basis from which you can put this particular leadership principle into practice.

Finally, the question may arise as to why this specific leadership principle should be practiced. The first reason, and the less important of the two, is pragmatic. Using this principle will turn you into a better leader and will thus make your team and your whole organization that much more effective and efficient in achieving its aims and goals. The second, and the naturally more important reason, is that the practice of charity—which is ultimately what giving is—is a Catholic imperative. And as a Catholic leader, you know that the teachings and the requirements of the Church are binding and forceful, thus necessitating their practice by all Catholics, which means that charity *must* be performed. So for these two reasons, *giving before receiving* is a leadership attitude worthy of being held and maintained.

It is no great shock or surprise, of course, that Jesus Christ epitomizes this leadership principle. Christ's whole ministry, as evidenced in the Gospels, is one long demonstration of giving rather than receiving. From His miracles, to His healings, and to His teachings, Christ gave to all and received from few. Indeed, as Jesus Himself said: "Foxes have holes, and birds of the air have nests, but the Son of Man has nowhere to lay his head" (Matthew 8:20, ESV). And though Jesus had no place to lay His head, and even though He could have received the entire world, as offered by Satan, Christ rejected the reception of such "gifts" and instead decided to give rather than receive. He gave of Himself. He gave of His blood. And He ultimately gave His life. Christ is a true incarnation of this specific leadership principle; He gave, in some way, at every time and in every circumstance. However, not only do we see this particular leadership principle expressed through Christ's life in its most intense, total, and perfect form, but it is also possible to see how Christ, in giving so freely and totally, simultaneously receives from those that He has given to. For Christ, as God, desires to freely save as many of His created creatures as possible. And by sacrificing Himself in such a totally giving way, Christ receives precisely what He desires, for it is through His sacrifice that so many saintly and loving human beings have freely chosen to give their lives to Him. Consequently, as a Catholic leader who is always guided by Christ, take care to give to those that you lead rather than receive from them, for just as Christ did, so should you do. And just as Christ was a loving servant to others well beneath Him in glory and power—even washing their filthy feet—so too must you be such a servant, which is a concept that perfectly encapsulates the old military adage that a leader's priorities must always be as follows: my mission, my men, and only then myself!

CHAPTER 7
COMMUNICATE STRATEGICALLY
AND KEEP YOUR FOLLOWERS INFORMED

EFFECTIVE, EFFICIENT, and engaging communication is both a skill and a goal of vital necessity for any leader. The need for clear communication is one of the pillars of organizational leadership, a pillar without which no organization can survive. For it is only through unambiguous communication of one form or another that it is possible for a leader to transmit his goals, intentions, and ideas to his subordinates. And it is only through communication that a group can actually *be* a group, for being a group requires individuals to be set towards a common purpose rather than simply being a random mix of uncoordinated and uncooperative individuals. Such purposeful cohesion can only be achieved through communication. Thus the need for *effective, efficient, engaging,* and *clear* communication, as well as the practice of it, should be one of the prime objectives of any leader. Indeed, as it is a truism that miscommunication—whether due to intentional maliciousness or unintentional inability—can not only cause general confusion about your mission, but can actually lead to the utter failure of the mission itself, then the idea that communication is an indispensible component of leadership cannot be overstressed. For example (and this example purposely seeks to demonstrate the criticality of communication to leadership), picture a General who, while leading a strategically superior army during the most crucial battle of a war, poorly communicates his tactical orders to his subordinates. Due to these multiple miscommunications, the various subordinate commanders maneuver their troops at the wrong times, and in the wrong manner, as well as into the wrong formations. From these mistakes, a sure victory—due to the General's superior army—suddenly turns into a tactical loss, which then transforms into a rout from the battlefield, with the enemy forces sweeping in and crushing the remainder of the General's army. The destruction of this army subsequently leads to the loss of the entire war, and this inevitably leads to the surrender of the General's whole nation. Even if such an example may seem stretched, it is by no means far-fetched. Battles have been lost for much less. For this reason, effective, efficient, engaging, and clear communication truly is of the utmost importance.

Notice, however, that we have *not* said that a leader's communication must be total or absolute or complete. This is a point that needs to be specifically noted, for it is also a crucial part of communication. This is because communication must be strategic if it is to be effective and efficient. And strategic communication requires more than the mere clear and concise communication of a leader's intentions, directives, and orders to his subordinates; a leader also needs to possess the knowledge and the wisdom to know *what* to communicate, *when* to communicate it, *how much of it* to communicate, *how to specifically* communicate it, and *when not* to communicate anything at all. Consider, by way of a thought-experiment, whether you would provide grave and secret intelligence to a subordinate you did not trust, a subordinate who may be a traitor to your very cause. Of course you would not provide him with such information, but rather you would withhold it from him, just as you would withhold intelligence from any kind of "Judas," unless it was your specific intention to misinform such a traitor in one way or another. And if you would not do so, even in a hypothetical thought-experiment, then how much more important is it that a leader on whom much depends does not do so? Hence, a number of different elements are integral to strategic communication, and thus are integral to communication itself, which by extension means that they are integral to anyone who wishes to be known by the designation of Catholic leader.

There exist three primary things that must be done in order for a Catholic leader to develop his strategic communication skills. The first of the tasks that a leader must do is to intimately know his particular strengths and weaknesses as they specifically relate to his communication skills. A leader must, as an example, be cognizant of whether he is stronger at speaking than he is at writing, and if he is, then he must also know whether he is a stronger formal speaker than an informal one. Indeed, a leader must be fully aware of a vast number of aspects related to his individual communication skills, abilities, and techniques. In my own case, for instance, it did not take me long to learn that when I was speaking to my soldiers or my superiors, I could not do humor. Cracking jokes to start off a speech just never worked for me, no matter what I did. No one would laugh, but every single person present *would* look at me with a puzzled expression on their face, as if they were expecting the already-past punch line to appear at any moment. It would always be a catastrophe! As such, I learned very quickly that communicating humor was a great weakness for me, and thus I minimized my use of this specific communication technique. This decision, furthermore, simultaneously reinforced the already existent communicative strengths that I possessed in my strategic tool-box, as the removal of humor necessitated that I use these other, stronger communication techniques more often. So every leader must be acutely aware of his strengths and his weaknesses in the strategic communication arena. He must also strive to employ his strengths to the maximum, while at the same time constantly training, developing, and working on his weaknesses in order to improve them to the greatest extent possible.

Let's move on to the second point concerning strategic communication. If a leader is to be a strategic communicator, then he must constantly ask himself the most common set of questions: who, what, when, where, why, and how. And in order to ask himself these common questions within the framework of strategic communication, the leader must ask them in the following manner (not in order of priority or importance):

- Who should hear this information?
- Who am I speaking to?
- Who will be able to hear and *find out* the information that I am providing?
- What should I *specifically* say?
- What parts of the information should I provide to which individuals?
- What communication method should I use to best present my message?
- When should I communicate the information that I need to communicate?
- When should I communicate the specific parts of my message within my overall presentation?
- When should I deliver my message in consideration of the full situational circumstances?
- Where should I deliver my message?
- Where should I place aspects of my message in relation to the overall narrative?

- Where should I place specific emphasis and force within my message?
- Why am I providing this particular information?
- Why am I providing this message in the manner that I am?
- Why am I providing this information to these particular subordinates?
- How will I deliver my message?
- How will I make best use of my communicative strengths?
- How will I ensure that my message has been understood?

All these types of questions—and note that this is by no means a comprehensive list—need to be asked and answered by the leader himself, even if only internally, before any type of communication between the leader and his subordinates takes place. Without a doubt, filtering your message through such a gauntlet of questions will truly serve to transform simple communication into strategic communication.

The third and final component of ensuring the generation of strategic communication, over and above just a simple form of communication, is planning and preparation. In essence, it means making use of the first two elements, assessing them, and subsequently combining them into a cohesive whole that can then be used for communicative purposes. This is the planning aspect of the third component. For as stated, in order to communicate strategically, we must first diligently and thoroughly assess and combine those two initial strategic communication elements (knowing our strengths and weaknesses as well as asking our questions), and only then should we map out and plan the overall thrust of our particular message. As leaders we are all required, therefore, not only to ask such questions, but also to prepare and plan our message around the answers to these questions as well as around our own communicative strengths and weaknesses. All three of these elements thus need to be completed in order to generate strategic communication, which is the key requirement of the particular leadership principle under discussion.

Yet simply knowing of strategic communication is not the only requirement of a leader, for such communication naturally needs to be employed if it is going to be of any use in keeping the leader's followers *strategically* informed, which is a perennial and never-ending task. Now, there exist a number of significant reasons why a leader should, at all times and in all situations, keep his subordinates informed. The most important of these reasons is that uncertainty, which stems from not being informed, breeds fear. And fear destroys morale, which is the lynch-pin of any organization. Thus keeping your subordinates "in-the-know" is intimately linked to the morale of those subordinates, and this is reason enough to ensure that you always keep those same subordinates properly informed. Furthermore, when looked at from the exact opposite perspective of this previous example, it is clear that as the maintenance of your team's morale is itself a necessary leadership task, then this requires you to do whatever is necessary to maintain that morale, which thus means keeping your followers informed. So, from both these angles, ensuring that your subordinates are informed is not just something that you should simply desire; rather, it is something that you must necessarily *do* in order to provide optimal leadership to your team.

The second reason to keep your subordinates informed is that an uninformed subordinate is a subordinate who spreads rumors, and rumors are like a vicious cancer that eats away at every aspect of a group, especially its morale. This means, quite simply, that all the points from the first reason are simultaneously applicable to this second one. But even further, an organization run amok with rumors is an organization run amok with rumors *about its leader.* Quite obviously, this is an undesirable state of affairs. And this, by way of an aside, leads to yet another reason to practice thoughtful, strategic communication. For if you do not do so, and thus neglect to discern who, what, when, where, why, and how you should communicate, then you yourself might be the very source of such rumors. This would be the *most* undesirable state of affairs, and it would undermine your leadership to the highest degree.

Finally, the third reason to keep your followers informed is because intelligence provides knowledge, and knowledge truly does provide its yielders with power and confidence. Not only does keeping your followers informed dispel fear, as in the first reason, but it positively and actively builds confidence and mental power. It makes your subordinates more secure, more resolute, and more prepared for any eventuality that may come their way. All three of these reasons are, therefore, more than adequate to completely necessitate keeping your followers informed via strategic communication. But this raises yet another question: What should you inform them of?

Ultimately, via strategic communication, we must keep all our followers informed of *everything* occurring within our organization, or relating to it. We may vary *how much* intelligence we provide to certain subordinates, or *when* we inform certain subordinates, or *how* we notify certain subordinates, but in the end, all our followers must be made aware of the goings-on within the entire team. In this way, you ensure informational fairness and equality—in keeping with the necessary privileges of rank and organizational hierarchy—for all your subordinates. Consequently, as an example of this idea, it is clear that while you would discuss the full and unadulterated details of a sensitive incident with your second-in-command, you would both very likely wait some time before discussing the same incident with your lower subordinates, and would simultaneously remove many of the details of the incident when informing those same subordinates of the occurrence. This would be strategic communication in action. And yet regardless of this, it is still possible to see how *all* your subordinates are informed of the incident, thus achieving your aim of keeping every one of your subordinates fully and completely informed. And, perhaps unexpectedly, we see all these aspects of strategic communication in Christ's own communication methods.

The method by which Christ communicates is always both striking and shocking. At times, Christ is abundantly clear in His message and in the manner by which He communicates it. At other times, Jesus is cryptic and hidden in His meanings, making His message clear only to Himself. Furthermore, Christ is selective in terms of when, where, how, and why He makes His message known, at times speaking to the multitudes and at other times only speaking to a select few. At times He speaks in parables. At other times Christ communicates with a plain tongue. And in the Gospel of Matthew we read one of the reasons why Christ communicates in such a manner:

> Then the disciples came and said to him, "Why do you speak to them in parables?" And he answered them, "To you it has been given to know the secrets of the kingdom of heaven, but to them it has not been given. For to the one who has, more will be given, and he will have an abundance, but from the one who has not, even what he has will be taken away" (Matthew 13:10-12, ESV).

And the Gospel of Luke reinforces this point: "And when his disciples asked him what this parable meant, he said, 'To you it has been given to know the secrets of the kingdom of God, but for others they are in parables, so that seeing they may not see, and hearing they may not understand' " (Luke 8:9-10, ESV).

From Christ's words, it must indeed be admitted that it is initially striking and shocking that Christ communicates in a manner that would lead many individuals to not fully appreciate what His message truly is. But such a fact loses its shock value when it becomes understood that Christ is communicating *strategically*. Jesus knows His strengths: preaching and speaking as well as communicating in parables, stories, and analogies. Christ has also answered the key strategic communication questions for Himself, as it is clear that He knows precisely why He is communicating in the manner that He does. He knows which people need His messages, and which people do not. He knows which of His messages is the most appropriate to His current audience. He knows where to communicate His specific messages. And He knows what messages to communicate depending on the circumstances that He finds Himself in. Finally, Christ plans and prepares His communication, for He provides the right message at the right time and in the right method. In all these respects, it is demonstrably certain that Christ engages in strategic communication, and He is extremely precise in how He chooses to do so.

In addition, even as Christ strategically communicates, He ensures that He keeps His followers and disciples informed. We see this throughout the Gospels, as Christ not only clarifies for His disciples the specific stories and parables that He does not explain to others, but He also provides those same disciples with original and unique information which is meant for them alone. Now, it may be true that Christ's disciples and followers are not cognizant of the full implications of the messages that they are receiving from Him, but this element is part and parcel of Christ communicating strategically. Thus, from both His strategic communication practices, as well as through His demonstrations of keeping His followers informed, it is more than apparent that Christ exemplifies this particular leadership principle, just as He does every other.

From a vast amount of vivid personal experience, I can also attest to the absolute necessity of strategic communication. In fact, such is the necessity of it that from the very beginning of my career I can think of countless stories demonstrating, in exemplifying fashion, the virtue of strategic communication. Yet I can, at the same time, recall a number of stories that denigrate this practice in the worst of ways. For example, I can remember having been hired by the military for less than a week and flying in, with over a hundred other new officers, to my first military base for training. However, due to a miscommunication in timings, when all of us landed at the airport, no one was there to meet us or to transport us to the base, many far miles away. So due to such a simple confusion, over a hundred officers were left stranded without support or assistance. Now, just imagine the damage that would have been caused if this had been a planned timing for something actually important. Or, as another example, I remember when on a large scale exercise, I and my fellow Platoon Commanders, as well as a number of other specialized military officers, sat to receive operational orders from our Major. We expected coherent and capable instructions as well as clear communication from someone of such high rank. Yet what we received, for the next hour and a half, was an incoherent mess of instructions, with our Major jumping back and forth between different sections of the orders. One minute he was explaining something as vital as what our overall mission was to be, and then the next minute telling us, experienced soldiers, that it might rain, so we would need to make sure that we all brought our raincoats. Now, to an individual who understands military orders—which are supposed to be extremely clear, ordered, and structured—it would be apparent that such a performance would be an utter mockery of the military orders process as well as a mockery of military communication in general. In fact, the orders were so disjointed and confusing that once they were complete, all the subordinate officers had to gather together a distance away from our Major and literally rework the entire plan without having him involved. We had to ensure that we all knew *what* was required of us and that we knew *when* it was required, because ultimately, from our Major's instructions, we had received none of these things clearly. Not only did this waste our time in the most extreme sense, but it truly and greatly undermined the trust we had in our Major, who was our leader. Quite literally, his leadership was heavily weakened due to his poor communication. And this weakening of his leadership prestige was never regained. Such is the importance of communication to leadership.

Lastly, I can remember examples from our Theatre of Operations in Afghanistan when I was deployed there, where certain less-than-vigilant military individuals would transmit intelligence in the presence of local hired Afghans who were of a questionable and uncertain sort. This, in turn, led to the enemy Taliban forces gaining intelligence on us that they immediately used to their advantage. And I do not mean this in the abstract sense. The Taliban literally gained enough intelligence to specifically mortar and rocket certain portions of our camp, targeting those buildings that they so recently learned were critical to our military efforts.

Yet these are only the less than exemplary illustrations, and as we should not leave this chapter with sour grapes in our mouth, it is also worth pointing out that there were actually many good examples that I remember as well. Indeed, in relation to the last example I just gave, I also recall that once we had learned of the treachery of those certain Afghans, the following action was taken: whenever an operation of strategic importance was being planned, all the required soldiers were quickly informed of the matter and all brought to a secure, locked-down location, thus creating an environment where the requisite intelligence could be received without the potential for betrayal from anyone. In this manner, we quickly learned *when* to communicate, *to whom specifically* to communicate, and *where* it was safe to communicate.

I also recall the vast number of orders, instructions, and directives that I received, from both superiors and subordinates alike, which were clear, cohesive, coherent, and comprehensive. And when such orders were effectively and efficiently given, they were indeed remarkable. Imagine, if you would, providing orders so clearly and coherently that over five thousand soldiers, commanding hundreds of vehicles and controlling tons of material, knew exactly what to do, how to do it, where to go, when to be there, and why they were doing it. I might also add that these soldiers knew all these elements down to the smallest detail. It was truly an impressive thing to see such accurate communication. And I even remember leading my own men into battle, where my communication, which was of the utmost importance, had to be ideally adapted to the situation. In some circumstances, when our stealth and our silence was the critical factor, then my combat orders, being communicated through hand signals only, had to be both as brief and precise as possible. Or when my men and I were fighting hard towards an objective (on exercise or otherwise), with the deafening sound of dozens of vehicles and the noise of explosions as well as the rattle of machine gun fire surrounding us, I would have to scream at the top of my lungs just to be heard, and yet my commands needed to direct and lead my men even in these conditions. And lead these men I did, providing distinct direction and driving my men onto and through the objective. But these instances of excellent communication could not have been achieved without understanding and employing *strategic* communication.

All these examples are thus simply meant to reiterate and illustrate the key point of this particular leadership principle: Always keep your followers informed via *strategic* communication. This means that your communication, in all its forms, must be clear. It must also be organized. It must, moreover, be planned. And it must be coherent, purposeful, concise, confident, meaningful, comprehensible, and precise. This also means that you must always deeply consider the message that you are providing. You must consider how to give that message, and how much of it should be given. Indeed, you must answer all those previously described key strategic communication questions in order to ensure that you are communicating effectively as a leader. And finally, you must consider the ultimate purpose of your message. To do anything less than all of this when communicating is to fail as a leader in general, let alone as a Catholic one. So mark each of these specific words and ideas well, understand them and absorb them, for they are the overall key to unlocking this most valuable leadership principle of strategic communication.

CHAPTER 8
GUIDE, TEACH, AND TRAIN YOUR FOLLOWERS AND YOURSELF

AT SOME POINT, all leaders become either incapacitated or are simply at a loss as to how to proceed in a given situation. Nowhere is this more evident than in the military, where a leader might suddenly be killed on the battlefield without a moment's warning. The same could be said of the early days of the Church, where a Christian leader could be martyred at any time, just as Jesus Himself was. Due to this harsh reality, leaders must ensure that they diligently train their subordinates in realistic conditions in order for those subordinates to gain the skills necessary to allow them to comfortably and confidently assume the role of leader when the need arises. And have no doubt that the need will indeed arise, and it will do so in the most difficult and unforgiving of circumstances. This is why your subordinates must always be ready to be leaders themselves. At the same time, you, as a leader, must also be ready to move on, for it may be that you will be required to step up and take on the role of your superior. In fact, it is near certain that at some point in your leadership career, you will need to fulfill the duties and responsibilities of your superiors, which means that you must know these advanced duties and responsibilities well before you need to complete them.

In the armed forces, an unwritten rule existed that every single military member needed to be able to competently complete the tasks and duties required at two ranks above his present level. In practical terms, this meant that a soldier who might currently be leading no one, such as a Private, needed to be able to fulfill the task of leading and directing eight other soldiers, a task normally given to a Sergeant. Or a Lieutenant Platoon Commander, normally leading approximately 30 people, would need to be able to perform the role of a Major Company Commander, thereby possibly having to lead and guide over 130 people. This idea of knowing the job of those individuals "two ranks up" indicates just how important the military takes the requirement to constantly maintain and improve leadership training and teaching.

Furthermore, consistently guiding, teaching, and training your subordinates to be leaders will simultaneously make those same subordinates better followers. This is because, through the understanding that your followers will gain of the tasks and duties that you are required to fulfill as a leader, they will be better able to appreciate your role when you are directing and commanding them from your position of leadership and authority. In having to do what their leader has to do, your subordinates will gain a strong respect for the extra hardships and additional responsibilities that being a leader entails, which will make them value their leader all the more. Additionally, your own advanced leadership training and education will make you a better sub-leader to your superiors, for the very same reason that it makes your subordinates better followers. Finally, as the technology, tactics, and tools of every trade naturally change and shift over time, it is necessary for every leader to instruct both himself and his followers in the use of these various new technologies, tactics, and tools. Indeed, for a leader, education must never stop, and any leader who does stop educating himself will soon flounder into incompetence and backwardness. These are, therefore, the primary reasons that every leader needs to ensure that he guides, teaches, and trains not only his subordinates, but also himself. And that is also why this specific idea is included within the ten vital leadership principles contained in this book. Yet each separate aspect of this specific leadership principle is unique in its focus and depth, and as such, each aspect of guiding, teaching, and training needs to be examined on its own.

To guide means to teach our followers through our actions and our example. It means silently teaching through non-verbal methods and deeds. This is why leading by example is so critically important for every leader, because doing so is not only a vital leadership principle in and of itself, but it is also a means of teaching your subordinates through your daily actions and activities. And thus a leader must always remember that his daily life educates, instructs, and tutors his followers, whether he wants this to be the case or not. But how is the *leader* guided? Who or what does he look to in order to provide himself with a guide?

A leader has two primary means of being guided and thus has two ways of being taught via this method. The first is to choose and follow a mentor, who is able to provide an example to the leader that he can pursue and emulate. In fact, one of the first things that my senior work peers recommended I do upon joining a specific military unit was to examine a number of high-ranking military officers and then choose one as a mentor who could assist me and provide me with a competent example to follow. And this technique is indeed an excellent means for a growing leader to learn and develop his own skills via the skills and example of someone more experienced and capable. The second method available to the Catholic leader, to ensure that he is constantly guided, is through the maintenance of his own Catholic vision as well as by holding fast to the very leadership principles found in this book. A Catholic leadership vision, as well as the overarching and timeless leadership principles found here, will always act as a guide that steers a leader and at the same time educates him by increasing his self-understanding and promoting critical self-reflection. Therefore, to be mentored both by another leader and by the leadership principles themselves is an excellent way for you, as a leader, to be guided in your own leadership development.

Teaching, unlike guiding, means education and instruction via verbal communication. It unavoidably brings forth images of a classroom or lecture, with a teacher standing in the forefront, instructing a large number of attentive (or, more likely, inattentive) students. And this is precisely the image that it should bring forth, because this is what teaching primarily is. It is classroom-type instruction, and it is an indispensible method for increasing both a leader's knowledge as well as increasing the knowledge of his subordinates. As a leader, you must ensure that from time to time, and as is necessary, you provide such teaching instruction to your subordinates. Whether it is to instruct them on a new piece of technology, or to teach them some new abstract concept that will be immensely beneficial to your organization if learned, or to simply provide them with a general knowledge presentation that will increase their overall awareness and skill, the teaching method of education is vital. Though it may be viewed by certain individuals as boring or outdated "school/bookish" learning, such objections are misplaced and unfounded. The fact is that for certain subjects, the classroom-style of education is the best means available to teach such topics and thus it should be the means that is used, rather than simply complaining about doing so. Furthermore, it should be added that the fact that this method of teaching brings forth images of a *formal* classroom, does not entail that this must be so.

CATHOLIC LEADERSHIP

There was many a time that I would informally gather all my soldiers together, even out in the cold and raining wilderness, and provide them with some classroom-type instruction on some new infantry strategy or new piece of technology that we had just received. As a result, such a style of informal instruction is most certainly possible in many different environments, as long as the leader is prepared for it and is competent in his informal teaching methods.

As with guidance, a leader must also continue to educate and teach himself. Whether it is through formal means via an educational institution or through informal and personal study, all leaders must remain in a constant state of self-teaching and self-schooling. In fact, a leader should always ensure that he is more educated and more knowledgeable than his subordinates, not so that he can be arrogant in his educational superiority, but so that the leader can use his advanced knowledge to assist and teach his own subordinates. His superior education and knowledge permits him to transmit that higher level of education and knowledge to his subordinates, thus improving their skills and ability in an overall and general sense.

As military officers, not only were we expected to possess a university education, but we could not be promoted to a higher rank without one. And the higher in rank you grew, the more advanced your education needed to be. Now, it should be immediately stated that this way of correlating education with career advancement was not a way of punishing or retarding certain individuals' career growth, but was rather a means of ensuring that no officer fell into a hole of mental stagnation and intellectual decay. To advance in your career, you needed to advance in your mind, and this was a responsible and intelligent guiding principle. Even at the lower level of the military officer rank structure, which is where I was located, all military officers were expected to complete various military-flavored academic courses in order to ensure that our writing skills, our intellectual problem-solving skills, and our thinking skills did not become static, sterile, and uncreative. Indeed, such a policy—whether instituted formally or informally—is sound, and should be adopted by any leader who wishes to extract the very best cerebral results out of his subordinates' intellectual work performance.

The more we sweat in peace, the less we bleed in war! This is, essentially, the motto of the training style of education. It means that the harder and more realistic that we physically train in practice, before the event that we are training for actually occurs, then the easier the real situation will be to deal with when it does occur. Training also means learning through a physical style of education; it is learning through the practical application of the theoretical knowledge that we have acquired from the other two learning methods. Now, not all professions or organizations necessarily need physical training, as many jobs in today's world are static, but the fact remains that for those professions that do require the completion of strenuous physical tasks, training is an utter necessity.

Training includes the creation of mock scenarios and practical exercises to test and develop a team's physical skills and practical abilities before that same team ever has to go out and test themselves in the real world. For example, before any soldier would be sent to Afghanistan or some other foreign location, he would be in training for months prior to his departure. And this training would be of the most realistic and intensive sort. It would attempt to mimic, down to the smallest detail, the real conditions that the soldier would experience in the overseas combat zone that he was being sent to. This, in turn, would prepare the soldier in the best manner imaginable, training him to overcome as many different situations and circumstances as possible. Without this training, the soldier would be in a much more vulnerable state than he actually is after having received it. And it is not as if this idea is somehow new or novel. Any soldier today would find his training, although different in detail, to be much the same *in principle* to the training of any soldier in the past, whether it is a Crusader Knight training before his long march to Jerusalem or a Roman Centurion preparing to fight under the banner of Constantine's Cross. It is, therefore, a leader's responsibility to ensure that the means, availability, and actual training of his subordinates occur as often and as realistically as possible.

Having examined these three aspects, we can now look to Christ to see them reflected back to us from Him. In His ministry, Jesus Christ not only educated those around Him, but He did so in the manner that we have studied here, through guidance, teaching, and training. As Christ's every action was sinless and perfect, and as He is the model for all Christians to follow, His entire life was (and still is) a living demonstration of guiding others through His deeds, dealings, and activities. And quite literally, no specific example in this case is even possible, for Christ's *entire* life was guidance in its most perfect form. Indeed, Christ not only guides, He is *the* Guide.

In terms of teaching, we often see Christ formally instructing His disciples and followers. His preaching is a direct and clear form of teaching, for such preaching presents itself in much the same manner as a teacher would present his instruction to a classroom full of students. On one occasion, Christ even *rebukes* Martha for not putting down her mundane tasks—mundane in comparison to the task of listening to Him—and attending to His teaching (Luke 10:38-42), all the while praising Mary for doing so. This incident demonstrates just how seriously Christ took this method of instruction.

With regard to training, it is clear that Christ also valued this particular educational method. For example, before He was crucified, Jesus sent forth His disciples to preach all over Judea, knowing that soon after His crucifixion, they would be required to preach to the whole world. This was an excellent form of training, for it allowed the disciples to hone their preaching without too much danger and while still in close proximity to their leader, thus realistically training them before they went out into the truly dangerous and far-flung reaches of the globe. So in Christ we see an appreciation of the fact that subordinates truly need all three elements—guidance, teaching, and training—in order to fully grow and develop as followers and disciples. Yet even considering these three elements, it is simultaneously true that ultimately, the one unifying theme of this particular leadership principle is that *continued education*, in all its various forms, is a necessary requirement for any organization and any leader. Remember this specific fact, and you will naturally remember that you must also always guide, teach, and train your subordinates and yourself.

CHAPTER 9
ALWAYS SHOW INTEREST, CONCERN, AND IMPARTIALITY

A LESSON THAT no reader of the Gospels can omit is that Jesus always exemplified the attributes of fairness, concern, and interest in the condition of those around Him as well as in the condition of those people in need. A leader must always demonstrate these three traits, for they are integral to solid leadership. By contrast, and in an opposing manner, it should be readily appreciated that literally nothing can erode the cohesion of a group faster than a leader that shows unjustified favoritism, or treats his subordinates like commodities rather than human beings, or displays no interest in the trials and tribulations of those that he supposedly leads.

Without expressing an all-encompassing interest in his subordinates, a leader will be at a loss to determine which subordinates are more skilled than others, which subordinates are skilled in which specific area of expertise, which subordinates are having personal problems that are affecting their work performance as well as which subordinates are causing tensions and problems within the group. These are only some of the reasons that being interested in the personal and professional lives of the people that you lead is utterly critical. Furthermore, maintaining an interest in something or someone—regardless of whether this interest is only maintained for professional reasons—is the only manner in which it is possible to gather *intelligence* on the thing or person in question, for you have to possess a strong interest in something before you will take the time to properly gather and analyze information about it. And as the second leadership principle discussed in this book was to gather intelligence, remain aware, and stay current, then this gives you yet another reason to maintain an interest in your subordinates and their activities. Finally, being interested in the manner required for this leadership principle is crucial not only in general terms, but specifically because as a leader you will be required to adjudicate in various matters between your subordinates, and to do so properly, you need to be aware of situational details whose discovery is totally dependent on your interest in finding them. They will not just appear to you; you will have to dig for them. This is simply an unavoidable reality of leadership. Nor is this an exaggeration, for on many occasions you will be called upon to act as judge and jury for a disciplinary affair involving one or more of your subordinates, the outcome of which can irreversibly change the lives of those followers.

When we think of Jesus Christ as the ultimate Judge, we can see this idea of interest developed to its most intense and perfect sense. For Christ the Judge of All Men is not only interested in some things that we have done, He is interested in *all* things. Truly, Jesus Christ will not only call us to account for some of the actions that we have taken, but rather, He will ask us to answer for every single thing we have ever done or thought, both good and evil. Now, this may seem beyond extreme, but it is actually the epitome of leadership and love, for Christ shows us that He is not only concerned about part of us, but all of us. Since He loves us completely, He is simultaneously and unavoidably interested in us completely. On the Last Day, Jesus Christ's total interest in every part of our being will be the greatest expression of His most perfect leadership and His most perfect love, even though we may understandably cower before it. And since, as Catholic leaders, we are to follow Christ to our utmost, then we should also follow the manner in which He expresses this utter and total interest in those that He leads.

Being interested, however, in a manner that correctly fulfills the requirements necessary to act as a judge and a jury for our subordinates, requires more than just interest, which is simply the first step. What it truly requires is an interest that transforms into concern. For although it is possible to show interest without showing concern, such an interest is insufficient for a Catholic leader. It is, furthermore, insufficient for a leader who wishes to be the most effective and capable that he can be. Interest takes you a small part of the way, but it is concern that takes you to the final destination, which is ultimately the destination that needs to be arrived at if you are to provide your subordinates with the care and attention they truly deserve. Whereas interest may arise from professional necessity or requirement, true concern can only arise from love. You must love your subordinates in order to show them the level of concern that does them justice as the followers of a Catholic leader. And though this may seem to be a tall order, it should be in no way difficult for individuals who are called upon to love even their enemies, which all Catholics are called to do.

Concern entails taking an *active* role in ensuring that whatever problem or issue that arises within your group is dealt with appropriately, and in a timely manner. It means staying on top of a problem until it is solved or a resolution is found. It means treating each problem or issue as new, even if you as the leader have dealt with a dozen other similar situations. And it means that you must always follow a modified version of the Golden Rule, namely: Always treat the problems and issues of your subordinates in the same manner that you would wish your own problems and issues to be treated. Or, to phrase it in a slightly different manner: Always show the same concern to your subordinates as you would wish to be shown to you. Understanding, accepting, and practicing this subset of the Golden Rule will put you in good stead towards ensuring that you are demonstrating the appropriate amount of concern for your followers.

Once again, we can return to Christ to teach us this aspect of leadership. For not only does Christ show total interest in us as human beings, but He also shows total concern. So much concern, in fact, that He knew that the only way in which He could express this perfect concern was to offer Himself as a sacrifice for mankind. The concern that Jesus Christ had for all His disciples, both past and present, was so great that He not only loved them, but He loved them undo death, much like a military leader who throws himself on top of a live grenade to save his men, but of an infinitely greater magnitude and nature. This is the type of concern that a Catholic leader must express. And though it is once again a tall order, it is a necessary one.

Concern, however, cannot overstep its bounds or be misdirected. It must indeed stem from love, but this love must be impartial. It must be fair and equal. It cannot develop or transform into favoritism, nepotism, or bias. True love is both blind and all-encompassing, while simultaneously being intimately linked to the idea of justice, and thus true love should naturally be impartial. This does not mean that a leader cannot express greater gratitude to certain followers over others, but rather that such gratitude must be linked to legitimate and warranted deservedness on the part of those specific followers. In essence, it is not a problem to reward a certain subordinate over and above all the others, but it is a problem to do so without reason or true merit on the part of this rewarded follower. The same holds true of punishment. To reward or punish a subordinate is not the problem; the problem is rewarding or punishing certain subordinates unfairly or with clear partiality.

Again we can turn to Christ to see this idea of impartiality in living form, for Christ will not only be the Judge of All Men, but He will be the *Just* Judge of All Men. Absolute justice, which Christ most surely provides, necessitates true impartiality and fairness. Even in His earthly ministry we can see that while Christ may have given different roles to His disciples, with some of these roles differing in their crucial importance, all His disciples were ultimately treated justly and impartially. The Apostle Peter, for example, was both rewarded by Jesus when he deserved such reward, and was then immediately disciplined by Christ when he deserved such punishment (Matthew 16:15-23). Indeed, Jesus, in judging all things fairly, was always impartial in how He distributed both His rewards and His punishments.

In my own career, I often experienced just how important this leadership principle was for ensuring and maintaining the morale and cohesion of my soldiers. In fact, I intimately remember how within the sub-groups of my platoon, which were led by my Sergeants, morale and effectiveness would be severely affected by a biased Sergeant—and I had more than a few of these—who would ruin the integrity of his team in only a few weeks of displaying such partiality and favoritism. And if I had not been either interested, or concerned, or impartial in my own dealings with such situations, then three things would have ultimately happened. First, if I was not interested in my men, I probably would not have even been aware of the situation itself. Second, if I had been interested but not concerned, then I most likely would not have taken sufficient or adequate action to remedy the situation. And if I had interest and concern, but not impartiality, then I would have just made the situation worse, either by ignoring the incident due to my favoritism towards the specific Sergeant or, if I did not like the particular Sergeant, then I would have overcompensated and punished the faulty Sergeant too harshly.

In another case that I recall, I had to deal with an unruly soldier who was on the verge of being booted out of the military altogether. And once again, if I had not been interested in my men, I would not have even known about this soldier's impending release, as it was being handled above my rank level. But because I was interested, I was able to inject myself into the decision-making process concerning that soldier's future. If I had not been concerned about my men, I would not have explored the soldier's situation, thus realizing that he had a vast number of personal issues that were affecting his work performance quite severely. I would not, furthermore, have even been concerned about his release specifically, if I was not concerned about him generally—which was a concern that arose simply because he was one of my soldiers who naturally deserved my attention and effort. Finally, if I had not expressed impartiality in dealing with this soldier's situation, then I probably would have simply washed my hands of him and his problems, writing him off as a bad and unredeemable subordinate. But, as I discovered after fully reviewing his past history, he actually was a redeemable soldier, and I did my best to see him retained as a member in my platoon. I was, I will admit, ultimately unsuccessful in my efforts. My decision to keep the soldier was eventually overridden by my own superior officer, but the point still stands: if I had not had interest, concern, and impartiality, I would not have been a true leader for this particular subordinate. Indeed, if I was not interested in his case, and was not concerned, or impartial to it, then how could I have legitimately called myself his leader? So these three elements are as necessary to leadership as they are vital.

Therefore, just as Christ is the perfect and just Judge who shows complete interest, total concern, and utter impartiality to those that follow Him, so must we as Catholic leaders strive to do the same. In addition, as leaders, we must also adopt the role of an earthly judge, a role that naturally entails the expression of interest, concern, and impartiality towards those being judged. And to truly realize just how important the *proper* adoption of such a role is to a leader, imagine having your life in the hands of a judge who has no interest in your case, no concern for your life, and no pretenses of being impartial towards you. You would rightly react in horror at being placed before such a person, so why should your subordinates feel any less horror at being placed before a leader who himself shows no interest, concern, or impartiality towards them?

CHAPTER 10
KNOW WHEN AND HOW TO BE A FOLLOWER

EVEN THE POPE answers to God! Indeed, from any angle, position, or profession, it is not difficult to understand the necessity of this particular leadership principle. Every single one of us, regardless of the position we hold or the profession we engage in, always has some type of superior to answer to—whether it be a direct superior, such as a supervisor at work, or an indirect superior, such as a customer and his demands. It is thus easy to recognize that there will always arise times when we must remove ourselves as leaders and become firm followers of the very leaders that lead us. This idea is made inherently clear within the military's organizational hierarchy, where not only are superiors of one type or another existent regardless of how high someone's military rank is, but the authority and will of these superiors is promoted and enforced through a rigid punishment structure that makes unwarranted disobedience both difficult and foolish. In such circumstances, you instinctively learn when to shut your mouth and simply follow.

I know from my own military experience that even though I had a great deal of autonomy and free decision making, I was simultaneously expected and required to follow the instructions and commands of my superior officers, of which there were many (both many commands and many superiors officers, that is). Although I was indeed a military officer and a leader of my own soldiers, and I was a leader in this sense every single day, I was, at the same time, often required to mentally remove myself from the position of being a leader, immediately shelve my pride, and humbly become a follower of the men that were leading me.

Now, this idea of still needing to be a follower may seem natural and easy to understand, and indeed it is easy to *understand,* but it is not necessarily easy to practice. For most leaders are in possession of quite forceful and driven personalities, and as such, the pride and desire to achieve objectives beyond their skill level and to lead in situations beyond their expertise are always prevalent in such leaders. These are, however, the very traits that make returning to the position of a follower, even if mentally accepted as necessary, quite difficult practically. Thus, the actual application of this leadership principle is much harder than the simple acceptance of its validity. Yet its importance cannot be over-emphasized, for on many occasions it is knowing when to follow and accept the orders of your superiors, rather than seeking to take command yourself, that will save you countless troubles and embarrassments. I can, even now, remember a number of occasions where this was the case for me; or rather, where it was the case that I forgot my place as a follower, and it was this forgetfulness that led to a great deal of pain, suffering, embarrassment, and annoyance for me and my men. In one instance, while on a military exercise, I was ordered by my Major to move to a certain location with my entire platoon, which was approximately five kilometers from my current position. The Major then proceeded to provide me with directions to the location, as navigation was difficult and he had previous experience with the area. But foolish me—being insulted that the Major would think that I, an experienced Platoon Commander, needed directions—I did not listen to my Major and simply dismissed him. However, after my entire platoon (with each man carrying over 80 pounds on his back) had already walked the five kilometers and had begun to dig in at the new position, I discovered, much to my dismay, that I had taken all of us to the wrong location, and that we were in fact a number of kilometers west of where we were supposed to be. Let me tell you, there is nothing that will shatter your pride faster, as well as nothing that will remind you to listen to your superior officer quicker, than having to tell your soldiers that you had just made them march to the wrong location with all their equipment, and had them dig trenches for a few hours at this wrong location, and *also* that we now had to march to the proper location and dig brand new trenches for a few more hours, all because you made an easily avoidable mistake that arose purely from your leadership avarice. After this episode and a few more of a similar nature, I learned very quickly when I needed to simply shut my mouth and listen to the advice of my superiors as a good follower does.

The Church, in large part, is the same as the military, and thus these previous points and stories apply just as easily to the faithful Catholic as they do to the military member. The Catholic Church's hierarchy, structure, and organization, in being so similar to a military one, easily makes use of this leadership principle and effortlessly demonstrates how valuable it is. For since its very foundation, members of the Catholic Church have all been followers in the ultimate and divine sense, but all members have also had to adopt the role of a follower at some point in time within the earthly and secular aspects of the Church and its relation to the world. For example, the lay-person is tasked to lead his family, but is also asked to follow the priest. The priest is tasked to lead his lay-people, but is also asked to follow the bishop. The bishop is tasked to lead his flock, but is also asked to follow the Vicar of Christ: the Pope. And the Vicar of Christ is tasked to lead the entire Church, but is also always and unceasingly tasked to follow Jesus Christ. So, in this manner, it is possible to see how even in its daily operations, the Church relies heavily on the idea that all its members must know when and how to become followers rather than leaders.

Even in Christ we see this leadership principle made manifest. Jesus Christ, although the true, whole, and founding leader of the Church while He walked on this earth, still subordinated Himself to God the Father fully and wholly. Every single Gospel account demonstrates that, at all times and in all places, Christ bent His will to be in accordance with the Father's will. Christ knew and acknowledged that regardless of His leadership, authority, and power on earth, He still answered to the higher power of God the Father. And thus Christ *the Earthly Leader* humbled Himself into the role of a faithful follower when necessary and appropriate.

Now, submitting yourself and becoming a follower of others is something that is done not only in the case of your superiors, but also for your subordinates. It is often the case that a leader must voluntarily relinquish control of his team, and must simultaneously transform one of his own followers into the temporary leader of that team. This may be done for a variety of reasons, and such reasons include, but are not limited to, the fact that one of your subordinates may have much greater experience and knowledge than you in a particular field of expertise, and thus would make a better leader than you when *specifically* dealing in that field. As the military has a number of different trades and professions, I know from my own career that there was many an occasion where I would be tasked to lead a group of soldiers to the accomplishment of a detailed task, but because the task was highly technical and skill-specific—skills and knowledge that I obviously lacked—I would readily assign temporary leadership of my team to one of my soldiers. I would do so because I knew that the specific soldier I chose could lead the group to the completion of this particular task in a manner that would be more effective and efficient than if I had led the group in the same task. Therefore, it was my concern to see the task accomplished as successfully as possible that led me to willingly demote myself to a follower's position. And this was a type of demotion that any true leader would happily take. Furthermore, yet another reason to let a subordinate lead in your stead is that certain situations may present a conflict of interest for you as the leader, so it is actually in your best interest to allow someone else to take the reins in these circumstances.

It must be made clear, however, that this leadership principle is not about losing control of the group, nor is it about losing your status as a leader. Rather, what you are doing in such a situation is *assigning* leadership to someone for a temporary period of time. You are assigning that leadership to them not because you cannot lead in this circumstance, but because as a leader you simply recognize that in the completion of a certain specific task, they are the better leader. It is still *you*, however, who makes the most effective and efficient leadership decision in that circumstance, which is to assign your leadership authority and power to a subordinate member of your team. In a certain manner, this is a form of delegation of tasks and a delegation of authority. But it is a unique form of delegation, because it is one where you, as the leader, are not only willing to delegate a task and the authority to complete that task to a specific subordinate, but you are simultaneously willing to *serve under and work for* that same subordinate. You literally become a follower of your newly assigned leader, rather than just an observing bystander who is simply standing on the side-lines waiting to retake the leadership reins. And a willingness to become such a follower is not a loss of leadership status, but a glorification of it, for it shows that you are willing to make the very best choices for the organization that you lead, even if it means relinquishing your own leadership for a time. Furthermore, never forget that you may take back those leadership reins at any point in time, especially if you see that your subordinate is less capable than you originally imagined. Therefore, your ultimate leadership authority, power, and command are not in jeopardy; you are still the *final* leadership authority of your group, just not the temporary one. Ultimately, never forget that while we, as leaders, can delegate our authority and power, we cannot delegate our responsibility.

Even within the Church, this idea is not foreign. Many a pope has submitted himself to the will, opinion, and the chastisement of Catholic saints, all of whom may have been lower within the official hierarchy of the Church, and thus subordinate to the pope, but were still understood as being worthy and capable of transforming and leading these popes in certain circumstances. Furthermore, even in the most basic of local parishes, it is clear that for many tasks that lie within the secular realm, such as Church finances, event coordination, and so on, the Church's priestly leaders naturally and willingly transfer their authority to various lay-people with expertise in such areas.

Even Christ, at times, would surrender His will and leadership to those that followed Him. Consider the wedding at Cana, where Christ performed His first miracle:

> On the third day there was a wedding at Cana in Galilee, and the mother of Jesus was there. Jesus also was invited to the wedding with his disciples. When the wine ran out, the mother of Jesus said to him, "They have no

wine." And Jesus said to her, "Woman, what does this have to do with me? My hour has not yet come." His mother said to the servants, "Do whatever he tells you" (John 2:1-5, ESV).

Christ then transforms water into wine, just as His mother wished Him too. So in these scriptural passages, so important to the Catholic understanding of Mary the Mother of God—who is merely a created creature in comparison to her eternal Son—it is possible to see how Jesus allows *her* desires to affect His will. Though it was ultimately Christ's decision, He allows Himself to be affected by the desires of His followers, even to the point of doing their will as if it were His own, as we have seen in this example. Consequently, Christ is becoming a follower and a servant via His own volition and choice, and if Christ is willing to do this, then there truly can be no shame or fault in our doing so as well. And not only would you be following Christ, but by becoming a follower and by delegating your authority to others in the interests of your team's overall organizational good, you also build the trust, confidence, and respect of your subordinates. Indeed, you build their self-reliance by showing them that you trust them with critical leadership tasks. You also build their confidence for you show them that if you are confident enough to entrust them with leadership authority, then they should be confident in themselves as well. And you build an overall level of respect, for you show your subordinates that they are more than just "mere" subordinates, but rather, they are budding leaders, all fully capable and able to take on leadership roles, and thus all worthy of respect and admiration. For these reasons and more, the leadership principle of being willing to become a follower when necessary is a principle that should not be trampled underfoot or neglected. To do so would be a detriment to every person that you lead.

CATHOLIC LEADERSHIP

Now, having shown this leadership principle to be both useful and practical, we need to articulate one final thing about becoming a follower: namely, the type of follower that you should be. As leaders, we all desire subordinates who are capable, knowledgeable, intelligent, hard-working, driven, initiative-taking, respectful, confident, faithful, obedient, humble, and energetic. In light of this, it is once again an excellent time—just as we partially did for the last leadership principle that we considered—to apply the Golden Rule: Do unto others as you would have them do unto you. What this means is that if we, as leaders, desire followers with the positive traits that were just listed, then whenever we act as followers ourselves, we should embody the very same positive traits to a maximal extent. And in support of this suggestion, I recall that Christ had quite a few harsh things to say about hypocrites, warning them most stringently as to what their hypocrisy would ultimately bring them. Perhaps we should take His warning to heart and realize that if we do not fully practice these positive traits when we act as subordinates, but demand those traits to be observed by our followers when we lead them, then *we* are the greatest hypocrites that there could be. Realizing this, we would have to wonder if we were actually Catholic leaders in the first place, for how could a willful and self-made hypocrite call himself Catholic? This is truly a pertinent question, for while we can simultaneously be striving-yet-failing sinners and Catholics, we cannot simultaneously be *willful* sinners and Catholics. This would ultimately be a contradiction in terms. So let us all recognize that to be Catholic leaders, we must not only understand when and how to be a follower, but we must understand when and how to be the very best follower that we can be.

CHAPTER 11
BE MORE THAN A FRIEND, LESS THAN A FRIEND, AND SOMETIMES JUST A FRIEND

A LEADER IS a great many things to a great many people. As such, a leader must often act as either a disciplinarian or a consoler or a dispenser of advice for the members of every closely-knit group with which he shares the bonds of sacrifice and hardship. Indeed, the critical skill that every leader must learn is at what times, and with what people, to play each of these different roles, for none of them can be avoided. Without discipline a group falls apart. Without consolation a team's collective heart becomes unnecessarily hardened. Finally, without advice a group's overall consciousness can never progress or move forward. It is, therefore, obligatory for every Catholic leader to learn the specific entailments of each of the three sub-elements of this chapter's overall leadership principle. And with each of these sub-elements being already uniquely articulated within the leadership principle itself, we can now develop an idea as to what each of these sub-elements require and entail.

To understand the idea of being more than a friend, we must imagine ourselves as mothers (and yes, I know that for all the non-mothers reading those words, this idea probably sounds quite strange, but it is actually a very effective way of achieving the requirements of this particular sub-element, and is thus being used specifically for that reason). A true and good mother is a blessing and a gift, for a mother's concern for us exceeds that of any friend by a wide margin. A mother guards her children and shelters them from problems and pain. She protects them, ensuring their safety. She is even willing to sacrifice her own life to protect her children. Such a mother is indeed more than just a friend; she is a person whose love for you is undying.

With this image of motherhood now firmly in our minds, it is much easier to appreciate how to truly be more than just a friend. Indeed, being a Catholic leader who *is* more than just a friend means being a leader who exudes kindness, care, and consolation. It means being more than just someone who is accessible to his subordinates for a private conversation or two, but rather someone who is actually available to be a true confidant and a real confessor for his followers. It means being a leader who maintains the utmost discretion and privacy concerning the men and women he leads. And it means employing what could best be described as a soft and gentle love with your subordinates when you are dealing with them. So in adopting this motherhood ideal, you quickly understand why you must look out for your subordinates' welfare, as well as care for their needs to a *maximal* degree, because a loving mother would naturally do so! You must also generate an atmosphere where this love and concern is easily felt and expressed, thus creating an area of comfort within which your subordinates know that they are free and safe to confide their issues and problems.

To fully understand why being more than a friend is a useful tactic for a leader to employ, a personal example is in order. About two years into my job as a Platoon Commander, I was approached by one of my soldiers with a personal problem that he wished to confidentially discuss. As I had been a Platoon Commander for this particular soldier for quite some time, I was well aware that I had already gained his trust to a certain degree. But just how much trust he had in me was soon to be revealed—much to my great surprise, I might add. In summary, the soldier was essentially requesting some additional time off of work due to family medical issues that had been on-going for a number of years. Now, it must be made utterly clear that this general fact is all that the soldier would have had to tell me; in the army, personal medical problems do not need to be known in detail, not even by a soldier's superiors. Yet my soldier, breaking into an emotional outburst, suddenly informed me that the problem was that he and his wife had been trying to conceive a child, but his wife had had over seven previous miscarriages, and she had just had another one. The soldier was requesting the additional time off in order to accompany his wife as she underwent a battery of different treatments and tests. And as he was telling me this, the soldier simply could not withhold the full flood of his pent-up emotions, literally begging me to give him the time off. It goes without saying that this soldier was granted whatever leave time he needed, a decision that any wise leader would have made. However, even over and above just granting him his request, it was clear that in this matter my soldier required more than just a leader, and he also needed more than just a friend. What he needed was a mother-figure. What he needed was someone to care for him and his needs beyond the level of attention that would be provided by a mere friend, someone that he knew would support him even in his weakest moments. And this is what I indeed provided, both listening to my soldier and allowing him to vent all his anger and sadness in an environment that was safe and compassionate. Now, for a person who is not intimately familiar with the military, this may sound like a strange thing for a military officer to do for one of his soldiers, just as it may seem strange for a leader to adopt the role of a mother-figure. But just as a family unit cannot be cohesive and strong without the virtues and values that a mother naturally brings to it, a military unit will also falter and fail if those same motherly virtues and values are not present in its leaders.

From this past example, it is additionally possible to glean when such a motherly attitude is to be used by you as a leader. Essentially, it is to be employed in the rare situations that demand the *utmost* care, love, and compassion due to a subordinate's deep hurt or severe personal pain. In such cases, adopting the motherly attitude is especially important since if this approach is *not* taken, then the subordinate will unavoidably lose his effectiveness as well as see his overall morale crumble. Further to this, it is also easy to understand *why* such an approach should be assumed. For it is an accepted truism that even the most morally corrupt of men love their mothers—which is why, incidentally, saying that a man would sell his own mother for something or other is traditionally understood as the greatest of insults—and as such, if you, as a leader, embody the same type of attitude as a loving mother would, then your men will love you in a similar manner as well. And just as nearly all men would do anything for their mothers, so too will nearly all your subordinates do anything for you if you act in a motherly way when the situation warrants it. This fact, in and of itself, provides more than ample reason to act as more than just a friend—indeed, to act as the subordinate's very mother would.

In Christ—whose own mother is also a stellar example for all Christian believers—we see a motherly instinct brought forth. In both the Gospel of Matthew and the Gospel of Luke, Jesus expresses how He wished to gather together all of Jerusalem, just as a "hen gathers her chicks under her wings" (Matthew 23:37, Luke 13:34, NIV). Such a metaphor is filled with the mothering ideal, and thus demonstrates this ideal from Jesus Himself. So in Jesus Christ we see that the motherly instinct, demonstrated in a concrete motherly attitude, is not only available to all people but is the optimal and most desirable attitude to adopt given certain personal circumstances and situations.

Note, however, that this motherly attitude should not be seen as some type of personal weakness. For just as a child will do anything for his mother, so too will a mother do anything for her children. Hearing of a mother lift a car off her children, or run into a burning building after them when even firefighters would not do so, are just a few examples of intense motherly power. Indeed, as opposed to being weak, mothers are the paragons of strength and power. But it is a strength grown from compassion and a power built on love—ideas that Christ would undoubtedly endorse. So remember that being motherly is not only necessary for leadership, but it is in no way weak.

Just as we may be called upon to fulfill a motherly role, so too may the fulfillment of a fatherly role be necessary. In fact, as leaders, we may be called upon to fulfill this latter role more often than the former. And to be a father figure is to be less than a friend, for a father is indeed not a friend but a father, meaning that he performs the role of family disciplinarian, controller, and authority. It is actually quite unsurprising that it is via the route of contemplating both how and why a proper Catholic father would act within his own family, that it is simultaneously possible to understand how and why such a fatherly approach is so well suited to leadership situations that require direct intervention and unwavering discipline. For being less than a friend to those subordinates that you lead, and thus being a father figure to them, entails the provision of hard love; it means providing a type of love that tells things straight, even if saying so is hurtful. It is a love that makes the right decisions, even if they are hard and unpopular. This is love that is not afraid to be harsh, if harshness is required. It is not afraid to criticize, if criticism is needed. And it is not afraid to punish, if such a course of action turns out to be necessary.

Personally, I can recall an occasion where a Sergeant, whom I knew from previous years, joined my platoon. The interesting thing was that I knew this particular Sergeant from my four years at the Canadian Military College, and during that time he and I knew each other well enough to christen ourselves acquaintances. I had always liked him, and I believe that he had similar sentiments about me. So when he arrived at my platoon, I felt quite fortunate and greeted him warmly. It was within a few weeks of watching him work, however, that it became apparent that his many years at the Military College had stifled his abilities as an Infantry Sergeant. He was both incapable of controlling his men as well as being unable to marshal the skills necessary to fulfill his various other roles as an Infantry Sergeant. Nor was he improving after being disciplined for his lackluster performance. To make matters worse, our entire unit was preparing for a deployment to Afghanistan, meaning that not only would this Sergeant be leading his men incompetently while at home, but he would also be doing so on an actual deployed operation. Something had to be done. So, in conjunction and conversation with my superior officer and other leadership staff, a decision was finally made. The Sergeant would be fired from his present position and moved elsewhere.

When my superior officer and I officially informed the Sergeant of our decision, he was both visibly shocked and deeply saddened, a fact that wore on me all the more due to my past history with him. He had in no way anticipated that such a course of action would be taken against him, and he was utterly flabbergasted that he was being removed. To add insult to injury, he even attempted to plead with us for his job back, and we had to quash this pleading both immediately and forcefully. Now, such an action was undoubtedly harsh, but it was also necessary and right. If my superiors and I had allowed the Sergeant to stay in his position as a leader of men, we would have jeopardized not only the Sergeant's well-being, but also his soldiers' safety as well as our own. So out of love and concern for all the parties involved, we had to take a course of action that *seemed* harsh and unloving, but ultimately was not, just as a father has to make decisions concerning his family that seem to be made without compassion, but actually spring from a deep and *hard* love. I might add, furthermore, that in the end, our decision worked out for all parties. My platoon received an excellent new Sergeant as a replacement, and we were made that much stronger for it. And my old Sergeant—who later confessed that he had been having serious marital problems during the time that he was in my platoon—stated that by firing him and moving him to a different position, we had actually given him the time and freedom that he needed to sort out various familial issues that had been plaguing him. This time for personal recovery, in turn, allowed him to eventually come back to our unit as a fully capable and committed Infantry Sergeant without problem or concern.

    I also remember an episode where, just after a number of our soldiers had been killed and wounded due to a mine-strike, I suddenly had soldiers in my platoon who were unwilling to go "outside the wire." In fact, I was approached about this matter by my Sergeants, who told me that some of the soldiers were requesting security duties within the camp so that they did not have to go out on patrol. Needless to say, I was rather livid. Such requests were, in essence, concealed cowardice, and I told my Sergeants as much. I further told them to inform our soldiers that if I heard any more requests of a similar nature, I would immediately take the requesting soldier and put him up on whatever military charges I could legitimately muster. Indeed, I told my Sergeants that I would ensure, to the maximal levels of my authority and power, that any soldier saying such things would be punished, without debate or discussion, in the severest of manners. Now, such statements may have seemed rough, but even the slightest smell of cowardice within military ranks needs to be snuffed out without remorse, lest it develops to consume and destroy group morale and cohesion. As such, I took the precise action needed to crush this building spinelessness before it grew any further. Yet I did so out of love, not out of a desire to punish. For as clearly stated, *if* I had allowed this cowardice to grow, then my whole platoon would have been put in danger. So my harsh discipline was borne out of love, not out of spite.

In Christ we also see such harsh love manifest itself when necessary. Look at His engagement with the disciple Peter, when Peter makes an unwise and seditious statement concerning the requirements of Christ's salvific mission:

> From that time Jesus began to show his disciples that he must go to Jerusalem and suffer many things from the elders and chief priests and scribes, and be killed, and on the third day be raised. And Peter took him aside and began to rebuke him, saying, "Far be it from you, Lord! This shall never happen to you." But he turned and said to Peter, "Get behind me, Satan! You are a hindrance to me. For you are not setting your mind on the things of God, but on the things of man." Then Jesus told his disciples, "If anyone would come after me, let him deny himself and take up his cross and follow me" (Matthew 16:21-24, ESV).

From this passage, it is clear that Christ is not afraid to be direct and harsh. Nor is He fearful about doling out discipline to His followers if they require it, or if they seek to hinder Him in the fulfillment of His mission. But as in my own examples, Jesus takes such rebuking action out of love, not from anger or hatred. He is harsh and unwavering precisely because His mission needs to be completed if He is to provide His love fully to the world, and thus it is out of love that He must discipline any follower who would stop Him from achieving that mission. So in Christ—who in the above passage is truly less than a friend to His disciples and much more like a disciplining father—we also have an illustration of both the necessity and the importance of hard fatherly love.

The final element to explore in this leadership principle is the idea of being *just* a friend. Indeed, even if we have already discussed the aspect of acting as a mother-figure and a father-figure, this still leaves out the final part of a nuclear family: the sibling. To be just a friend to those you lead is to be a brother or a sister to them. It means demonstrating the type of love that a sibling shows. It is a love that is simply willing to listen if that is all that is requested, but it is also a love that is willing to provide advice if that is what is desired. It is a love that is willing to help if that is what is asked for, but it is also a love that is willing to let the other person determine things on his own if no help is requested. It is a love that is willing to be as close or as distant as the subordinate desires or requires. And it is a love that will tell a subordinate precisely what he needs to hear, but without judgment or castigation, because it is a form of affection that is not overly concerned about caring for the subordinate (as a mother is), nor interested in disciplining him (as a father would be). It is the middle road.

Jesus called His disciples friends (John 15:15) and this fact teaches us a great deal about the type of love that was being conveyed through such friendship. For even though Jesus Christ was God Incarnate, and thus infinitely greater than His disciples in all respects, He was also willing to call them friends. He was willing to talk with them, eat with them, sit with them, and treat them as worthy of being His associates. In the same manner, as a leader, even though you ultimately possess an authority and command which places you above your followers, you must emulate Christ in showing those same followers that you are also their friend. Just like Christ, you must be willing to talk with them, eat with them, sit with them, and treat them as your peers. In so doing, you express your love for them by demonstrating that, although you are indeed above them in power and authority, you are *not* above being their friend. Remember, your followers may be subordinate to you, but they are not *inferior* to you. Without a doubt, they may be your friends even as you lead them.

In all these areas, therefore, it is clear that the key component to this leadership principle is love. A leader's love for his subordinates is applied in all these different areas, yet the *method* by which this love is provided is the key difference between them. It is a type of love that must span the spectrum of familial affection; it must include the love of a mother, and of a father, and of a brother or sister. Through the transmission of such different types of love—as long as they are used selectively and appropriately given the situation—a leader will gain love in return. Such a love will create bonds stronger than any other, and such bonds will hold an organization together even in the most dire of circumstances. Many of these bonds will be so strong as to only be broken by death, and a group with such strength and cohesion will be formidable beyond belief.

As Catholics, we are already commanded and instructed to love, so the idea of needing to be a loving leader is in no way an unexpected task. In fact, since we are commanded to love others just as much as Christ did, and to do so with our enemies as much as with our friends, it is clear that in our daily lives we should already be engaging in the skills required by this particular leadership principle. Extending those skills to the leadership domain is thus no great feat. So remember, through the select application of different styles of love, be more than just a friend if required, be less than a friend if needed, and sometimes just be a friend.

CHAPTER 12
BE PREPARED TO TAKE A STAND
AND IF NECESSARY TO STAND ALONE

THE CROSS: an instrument of pain, torment, and death. An instrument upon which Jesus Christ, for both ourselves and our sins, freely allowed Himself to be hung. An instrument that ultimately perpetuated upon Him the greatest of agonies: separation from His Eternal Father. And an instrument that Jesus Christ knew He had to submit to, a submission He planned for, accepted, and willingly went out to seek.

It is easy for us now, as Christ's followers, to both admire Jesus' tenacity towards the necessity of the Cross and the free-willed choice that He made to accept its painful fate, yet there is a most profound and important leadership lesson to be taken from Christ and the Cross. Indeed, this lesson, or more accurately a principle, is one that is utterly necessary to accept and acknowledge as a Catholic leader, and it is one that is exemplified by Christ upon the Cross. It is the leadership principle that every Catholic leader must always, and in any circumstance, be prepared to take a stand for what is true, right, and good. And if necessary, that same leader must be prepared to stand completely and utterly alone, no matter the onslaught that he stands against.

In articulating this idea, it is thus easily understood both how and why Christ teaches and demonstrates this principle in living action. For not only was Jesus Christ abandoned by those followers whom He held to be most dear, He was also given the opportunity to deny Himself and His earthly mission, thus freeing Him from a future that necessitated the Cross. Yet Christ refused to cower or falter. In knowing of the necessity of the Cross and the necessity of His suffering and death upon it, Jesus Christ essentially, and with unending fortitude, took a stand for the mission that He knew He must complete. Even though He was abandoned by all and betrayed by some, Christ stood as firm as a rock and never wavered in the completion of His necessary aim. In this manner, Christ truly embodied the leadership principle currently under consideration.

The question that arises, however, is why? Why must the Catholic leader be prepared to take a stand? And why should he even be prepared to stand alone if required? Although perhaps obvious to some, the answers may most certainly not be clear to others, so it is crucial to address these issues.

Perhaps the simplest manner of answering these questions is via another quick query: If the leader will not take a stand, who will? Or, to be more precise: If the leader will not take a stand, who *should?* Indeed, as it is the leader who is ultimately responsible both for establishing the aim and goal of the group he leads, as well as ensuring that that goal or aim is met, then he is simultaneously the one who must stand for that same goal or aim when all others fail to do so. Imagine, if you will, that a military battle is about to occur. The military commander, having organized the plan and established the defensive position that is about to be engaged by a massive enemy force, suddenly wavers, and then turns and bolts to the rear, leaving his men behind. Could anyone ever fault any of his soldiers for dropping their arms and doing the same? Of course not, for it is the commander who must always be the first to take a stand for what must be done, and if necessary, to remain standing until the bitter end. This is why it is incumbent on any leader to know, understand, and be ready to stand firm till the very end of his mission—even if that means the end of himself—if that is the necessary requirement for the accomplishment of the right, true, and good aim that was originally chosen and fought for. It is thus clear that taking a stand, at some point in time, is indeed a necessary leadership task, but now we must explore what exactly taking a stand entails.

While it is easy to see the applicability of this leadership principle in such cases as Christ and the Cross, or in a military setting where a leader taking or not taking a stand for his mission can either make or break the entire military endeavor, it is not necessarily that easy to see how this leadership principle applies for more commonplace (although no less important) leadership settings. But these more drastic leadership examples are actually just representative of an overall concept and idea that underlies all leadership situations, which is that all leaders have something to lose. And this is what is ultimately linked to the idea of taking a stand, for taking a stand as a leader—regardless of whether that stand is taken in a mundane setting or the most extreme one—means being willing to sacrifice aspects of yourself for the mission that you have chosen to pursue. It means being ready to sacrifice those important elements of your person and profession—such as your professional standing, your professional respect, your monetary compensation, and other things—in order to stand up for the accomplishment of your chosen goal. As such, it is clear that taking a stand is a leadership principle that you can fulfill regardless of your leadership situation, and regardless of your leadership prominence, and also regardless of the number of individuals that you lead. As a leader you will always have something of your own that can be lost, and thus, in taking a stand, you will always have put something "on the table" to be lost. Everyone thus has the ability to take a stand, for everyone has something to lose through taking that stand, even if all you have left is your own life (which is not meant to debase the worth of your life, but rather to say that even though every single other thing may be taken from you, you will still have your life to lose even when everything else is gone).

If everyone, therefore, can take a stand, and if the leader is the one who is first and foremost required to do so if the situation warrants it, then it is furthermore imperative to understand when such a stand should be taken. Taking a stand for what is right and moral does not mean possessing a rigid mentality that does not accept change or is unwilling to contemplate retreat. In fact, in many cases, it will be necessary for the leader to take a stand *in order to* change the minds of his own subordinates, or in order to force them to retreat—which simply means the abandonment of a mission or goal for another—when they do not wish to do so. The key element of when to take a stand, therefore, does not revolve around being rigid in your ideas or of never retreating, but rather rests on the issue of criticality. Indeed, knowing when to take a stand is intimately connected with knowing what goal or aim is critical and indispensible to your overall vision and mission as a Catholic leader. It is easy to illustrate this idea. Think again of a military commander, but one who in this case organizes a military action that, although helpful to his war effort, is not critical to it; thus, when a change to his overall battle situation occurs, he re-evaluates his position and retreats from it, changing his mind. In such a situation, where a certain task may be important but not vital, there exists no over-arching necessity to stand firm in one's decision, and it is as intelligent to change one's stance as to hold it. By contrast, if we imagine the same military commander planning an operation upon which the whole war effort depends, and which would be instrumental in changing the course of the entire war, then it is clear that in such a situation the military commander must be prepared to stand firm in his vision and hold steadfast to his mission, regardless of the pain or sacrifice required to do so. In the same manner, it is possible to understand how Jesus Christ's healing of one individual over another, or His preaching to one group of people over another, may not have been critical to His earthly mission, and thus He would not have necessarily been adamant about selecting a specific course of action in *such* situations. The Cross, however, is an element of the uttermost criticality to Christ's mission, so it is clear how Christ could do nothing but take a stand on the Cross, for His entire redemptive mission wholly depended upon Him doing so. Thus, the centrality of the goal chosen, and its criticality to the overall mission, is the key facet used in determining which situations warrant taking a stand against anything and everything, and which situations do not warrant such a stand.

With a number of key questions about this specific Catholic leadership principle now answered, a few still remain, for it is essential to address not only when to take a stand, but also against whom to do so. And this is perhaps one of the most surprising, and unexpected, of the aspects of this particular leadership principle, for every Catholic leader must understand that, at some point in his leadership career, a stand may need to be taken against *everyone!* Truly, as strange as it may sound, a leader must be ready to stand against all individuals that surround him. The leader must be ready to stand alone against his subordinates if they fail to stand with him and if they abandon him in the fulfillment of his critical mission, as was the case with Christ and His Apostles. The leader must also be ready to stand alone against his superiors if they fail to stand with him in promoting what is good, right, and true. And the leader must of course be ready to stand alone against *any* adversary, if those adversaries attack the leader's mission or seek to retard his progress towards a critical goal. In this way, it is possible to see that all the people who surround us as leaders may, at one point or another, need to be stood against. You can never assume or expect that this will not be the case. Linked to this, remember that some individuals may even stand against you, and depending on the circumstances—such as if you are acting immorally or are being grossly ineffective as a leader—they may be warranted in doing so!

Now, it is all well and good to continuously intone that this particular leadership principle is a necessary one (meaning that it is one that must be regularly employed by any Catholic leader worth his salt), but it is also crucial to provide the steps that can be used to develop this principle in small ways, thus slowly preparing and conditioning yourself for a time when it is fully needed. From a Catholic perspective, the first element that is needed in order to generate the courage necessary to take a stand is the understanding that Catholicism holds truth. By remembering this fact, you are provided with the knowledge that ultimately, as a Catholic, you stand on *the* pillar of truth, and truth is always worthy of being stood for. You are also provided, through the acknowledgment of this fact, with the remembrance that the will of God will ultimately be done in all things, and that God is behind you. Such an understanding *will* provide you with the courage required to take a stand when necessary. Indeed, courage is the first and most crucial ingredient for the fulfillment of this specific leadership principle, and in the end, the courage to stand in some of the direst situations can only come from the Lord Himself.

CATHOLIC LEADERSHIP

The second method of strengthening our ability to take a stand is to do so in small and less crucial areas. I know that we have already spoken of less important leadership situations being ones where we did not necessarily have to stand up for our goal or mission, but the fact is that in terms of *building* our leadership courage, such less crucial leadership situations present an ideal means to practice this leadership principle in small ways and thus develop a consistency in doing so. Note that this does not mean that you should take a firm stand as a leader in a minor situation where taking such a stand may actually cause harm or damage to the group. Rather, there will arise situations of minor overall importance that nevertheless warrant taking a stand for your position, and thus these situations present the ideal opportunity to develop your skill in taking a stand and facing the onslaught that follows. Therefore, a preponderance of Godly courage, coupled with previous practice, are the keys to standing firm for what is true, good, and right, regardless of the dangers that may come from doing so.

Finally, I can say from my own experience just how vitally important this leadership principle is, and I do not say this lightly. I remember that on one occasion, as a new and young officer, I consulted with my closest subordinates concerning a certain delicate matter involving my platoon, and ultimately made a command decision in favor of my platoon, but against the "recommendation" of my superior officer. This was not to my superior's liking. Standing at attention—straight and tall—I was eventually brought before my boss to answer for my decision and, furthermore, to answer whether or not I had made my decision alone. And there, standing at attention in front of an extremely angry boss who was screaming at me, the spittle from his mouth bouncing off my chest, I was indeed alone. Yet alone I decided to stand, for as the leader in that situation the buck ultimately stopped with me. Even though I had consulted with my men, the decision was ultimately mine, and thus I knew that although I could blame my subordinates and pass some of the punishment onto them, what I actually needed to do was to stand alone and take *all* the blame that was about to come. And so I did, taking the full brunt of my boss's wrath, which led to formal administrative punishment being taken against my record, a blemish that would follow me for the rest of my military career. Eventually finding out what I did, I can tell you that my subordinates appreciated it in a way that is difficult to express. Through my actions, they understood that I would stand for them, even to the point of serious detriment to my own career.

Yet do not think that this was a one-way street, for I remember many other instances where I had to stand against my own subordinates and support a sound and necessary decision that my superior had made, but one that my subordinates found to be undesirable. And if you think staring down an angry boss is difficult, it is certainly no more difficult than doing the same thing against thirty disgruntled soldiers. But those same subordinates respected me for doing what I did, even if they did not like it. And how much more so will this be the case for the Catholic leader, who must lead and guide others in the already hard teachings of the Church, teachings that are by no means popular even with other Catholics, let only non-Catholics! The Catholic leader may not be liked for doing this, but he most certainly will be respected.

So always be ready to stand for what is right, true, and good. And in this world, even be ready to stand alone, for in doing so, you will actually have Christ standing with you!

CHAPTER 13
BECOME THE LEADERSHIP PRINCIPLES

"I SHOULD HAVE had my stomach pumped." Through the thickness of my foggy mind, I unintelligibly mumbled these words over and over to myself as I retched, yet one more time, into the filthy toilet bowl of some random, nondescriptive roadside café. The seemingly endless projectile vomit was as powerful as it was disgusting, and I could do nothing but let my body take control of the faculties that my mind and will would normally steer, thereby allowing that same body to finish expelling all the foreign materials from its gut. There was no doubt that I was suffering—to the point of, quite literally, sweating alcohol out of my skin pores—but ultimately it was a freely chosen and self-induced suffering, so any sympathy that I might have normally felt for myself was absent, replaced only by shame and humiliation.

The night before, we had just been released into the big city—the exact name of which shall remain undisclosed—for a 24-hour leave from duty, after weeks of tented living out in the wild during which we conducted advanced military exercises. Not only had we been out in the wilderness for over a month already, but we would be returning for another number of weeks after this 24-hour furlough was finished. And all this meant that every single soldier would surely strive to make the most of this brief and fleeting respite, and make the most of it I, most definitely, had planned to do!

Arriving in the city via chartered bus, my platoon and I had decided that before dispersing to the four corners of the earth, where each of us could enjoy our time off in our own way, we would partake of a communal platoon dinner at one of the fine local restaurants. And as the vast majority of soldiers are wont to do, once we sat down to order our meals we all started drinking; and when I say that we were drinking, I mean that we were *drinking!*

So in this situation and circumstance I found myself. Now, I must admit that I cannot remember if it was due more to pride or stupidity—most likely a combination of both—but I do remember that right there, in that restaurant, surrounded by the very soldiers that looked to me for leadership, example, and guidance, I decided that I was going to out-drink them all. And I decided that I was going to do so in the most dramatic of fashions. To that end, I beckoned to the server that I would like *ten* vodka shots brought to my table, which I would drink immediately upon arrival, one right after the other. Within a few seconds of my saying this, the entire platoon had heard the news, and all my soldiers gathered around my chair. Surrounded by them, I suddenly realized that there was no way out. I was committed.

The ten shots of vodka arrived, the harsh liquid swirling in the small shot glasses as the server placed them, one by one, directly in front of me. And then, without hesitation, I downed every single one of them in fewer seconds than there were shots, ten shots in less than ten seconds. The hooting and hollering of my troops was deafening, and they loved the little show I had just put on. They loved it so much, in fact, that about five minutes after this first performance, they purchased me five shots of tequila, which I "dutifully" forced down my gullet just as fast as the first ten shots of vodka. And then, a few minutes after this second round, yet another two shots of vodka were purchased for me, which I once again pounded back as quickly as I could.

At this point, the novelty had worn off, and my soldiers dispersed to their individual tables, even though a few of them did approach me and told me that they had never seen anyone drink so many shots of hard liquor so fast before. It was a "one of a kind" show, they said. Now, this should have been my first warning, because every soldier in my platoon had seen an enormous number of people drink before, and drink *hard*, so if I truly was unique in their eyes, then this was a uniqueness that surely came with some not-so-desirable consequences. And sure enough, though fully capable, coordinated, and coherent for a miraculous 30 minutes after the drinking session, it was as I got up to go to the bathroom that the alcohol hit me like a proverbial ton of bricks. I fell over my chair and had to bounce back and forth off the walls of the hallway just to make it to the bathroom door. The worst, however, was yet to come, for it was after I exited the bathroom that my conscious mind blacked out till the sun came up the next morning, over twelve hours later.

I say my conscious mind blacked out because I was later told that I was still able to stumble about and follow the group, and to support this claim, I must admit that there were indeed brief moments where I would awake from my alcoholic delirium and realize that I had just been carted along by my soldiers to either a new bar, or another dance club, or their hotel room. I had become, essentially, a nearly uncontrollable dead-weight and a stupor-induced burden, being carried around and tolerated by my soldiers for the same reason that a family tolerates the family drunk: not because they want to, but because they do so out of a sense of familial duty. In like manner, I was a *soldierly* duty that the men in my platoon took on grudgingly, and they cared for me until we once again boarded the bus for our return trip the next morning. And it was during that morning bus ride that I screamed at the bus driver to stop at the first random café he passed, even though no one else wished to stop, because I most desperately needed a "coffee." Of course, what I actually needed was a place to puke, and that is how I wound up hunched over the café's toilet, as described at the beginning of this story.

I did not fully recover from that drinking episode for two whole days, and I can remember that my leadership and decision making during that time was of questionable quality. Although my soldiers did not say anything about the matter after it happened, it was clear that something was lost in their eyes when they looked at me. Though they had thought it funny and fun at the time, it slowly dawned on them that what I had done, I had done as *their* leader, and they had expected more of me. This incident did not destroy my working relationship with those particular men, but it most definitely weakened it, especially with the senior soldiers that knew I should have acted better. I had—and there exists no way to mitigate or "sugar-coat" this fact—failed my men, and I had failed myself. I failed to be an example. I failed to care for my men, instead making them care for me. Through my actions, I failed to teach my men the discipline and control of a leader. I failed to *give* to my men, and instead received from them, for it was they who had to give me their time, patience, and energy. In sum, throughout this entire episode, I failed to demonstrate every single leadership principle that we have discussed, and such a failure was catastrophic, not only from a leadership point of view, but from the Catholic one as well. Truly, in this particular case, I had failed to live up to and maintain any of the leadership ideals, let only any of the religious ideals, that I held. For how could I, as a Catholic, have allowed myself to engage in such behavior? I had, quite simply, failed in every imaginable respect.

Now, the question is, why have I told this story? Why have I described an event that is, to me, as shameful as it is pathetic and disgusting? The reason is that this example, more so than any other, demonstrates my utter failure (and demonstrates the consequences of that failure) to follow the final and most important leadership principle: That of *becoming* the leadership principles. If leading by example and remembering to always be a leader was the most crucial leadership principle among the first nine principles considered, then this final principle of *becoming* and *embodying* all the principles is the most critical from an over-arching perspective, for it ties together all the others and is thus applicable across the entire leadership spectrum.

Beyond a shadow of a doubt, you, as a leader, will soon understand that you are a leader at all times, in all places, and in every situation. A leader will always be observed and will always be assessed by those that know him as a leader. Furthermore, any leader may be called upon, at any moment, to lead in a situation that is both unplanned and not prepared for, and thus the leader can ultimately *never* stop being a leader, for he cannot simply switch his leadership skills on when the moment calls for it. Indeed, the leader needs to *be* a leader, not just act as one when he plans on it. Anything less than a total embodiment of the leadership ideals is simply a facade that will eventually fade and crack, showing the lack of quality and the lack of true leadership that lies underneath the glossy surface. And it is for these reasons that the leadership principles must be subsumed into your character, and must become instinctive and natural, if you are to be the leader that your Catholic faith calls you to be. The fact that we hold to the Faith, furthermore, necessitates that we embody these various leadership principles, for they are indeed principles that not only apply to, but stem from, our Catholic faith. As such, they are principles that we, as Catholics, should be practicing regardless of our leadership status. Finally, as demonstrated in the rather unsavory personal story provided at the start of this chapter, failing to uphold, employ, and embody these leadership principles in all situations, even those situations where your leadership does not seem necessary, can truly lead to a loss of your standing, respect, and leadership status in the eyes of the individuals that you lead. And too many of these types of failures can lead to a permanent loss of respect and admiration, thus unofficially removing you as a leader in the eyes of the majority of your subordinates. This is why, as Catholic leaders, we must become and embody the leadership principles; we must live them daily and exemplify them fully, just as Christ did.

Jesus Christ, as always, is the personification of this principle. For as Christ was sinless and perfect, and as we have demonstrated that Christ employed the very leadership principles that we have discussed, then Christ naturally and inevitably embodies these leadership principles to a total degree. Christ cannot but be the perfect leader, and thus cannot but give us a perfect example of the leadership principles that we have been exploring. Through all the Gospels, it is easy to note that in terms of striving forward towards His ultimate goal, Christ never fails or falls. He never stops leading His disciples, no matter the situation or the circumstances. He never takes His leadership "mask" off, for He has no such mask. He *is* what He preaches. And He *is* leadership.

It is through this understanding of Jesus Christ as the embodiment of leadership that it is possible to appreciate how to *become* the leadership principles. For while it is well nigh impossible to remember all the details of these specific leadership ideas, not to mention keeping them in the forefront of our minds from moment to moment, there is a simple way to accomplish this goal of embodying the ten principles: pick up your Cross and follow Him. It is through remembering, learning, praying, and asking for the support of Jesus Christ that it is possible to embody these most important Catholic leadership values. It is through following, applying, and practicing Christian ideals, which have been provided and exemplified by Christ, that we can slowly integrate these leadership ideas into our very natures. And it is through striving to be as Christ-like as possible that we shall gain the ability to be Christ-like leaders.

By contemplating how Christ, as well as the various saints that followed Him, would act in any given leadership situation, it becomes possible to understand how an individual can always remember to embody the leadership principles expressed here, even if he does not remember them specifically. Following Christ *is* following the leadership principles. The two are synonymous in the same way that following Christ *is* the same as following truth and perfection, and we must always strive to be perfect, just as our Father in heaven is perfect (Matthew 5:48). And in striving for this Christian perfection, we will simultaneously strive for the perfection of the ten Catholic leadership principles. Indeed, in following Christ's example, we follow the example of the world's most capable leader, and there could thus be no better way to become a leader than to follow the leader of leaders, and the king of kings. So follow Jesus, and the Catholic leadership principles shall, with a certainty drawn from the promise of Christ Himself, become yours!

CHAPTER 14
CATHOLICISM AND LEADERSHIP STYLES

THEY WERE experienced soldiers. They were technically and technologically specialized soldiers. They were "newbies" who were still wet-behind-the-ears. And they were battle-hardened veterans. They were, in essence, men and women of all types: experienced, inexperienced, specialists, generalists, leaders, followers, veterans, and others. Men and women of every stripe, skill, ability, and age: these were the very people that I, as a military officer and leader, had the distinction of commanding. Indeed, imagine not only such a mix of individuals, but also imagine leading them, and leading them well. These were the individuals that we, as the leaders of our soldiers, needed to guide, shepherd, and manage. And therefore, these were the individuals for whom we needed to tailor and adapt our overall leadership style, approach, and method.

Yet such varied military leadership is in no way different from the leadership necessitated in any other professional field. All leaders are expected and required to lead a diversity of subordinates with vastly different skill-sets and uneven levels of experience. In fact, such varied leadership is as required for the Catholic leader as it is for the military one. The Catholic Church, with its clearly defined hierarchy and vast array of specialized sub-professions, clerical roles, and organizational responsibilities, is thus an entity in which every leader will be faced with the task of leading a wide assortment of different individuals, all of whom possess varying degrees of expertise and knowledge. Therefore, the concern of employing an effective and efficient *style* of leadership for a given situation or circumstance is as pronounced for the Catholic leader as it is for any other.

So how do we achieve this goal of adapting and adjusting our leadership approach in order to provide the most suitable and successful leadership for a given individual or group? How do we properly tailor our leadership style in order to maximize our efficiency and effectiveness in a given situation or circumstance? And how do we do this as Catholic leaders, who of necessity and desire must develop their leadership methods in light of the teachings and direction of the Church?

Leadership approaches and styles
Anyone who has ever studied the topic of leadership and management will know that the subject of leadership styles or approaches is an issue that can occupy both a great deal of time and can simultaneously lead to a great deal of confusion, argument, and uncertainty. This is due to the plethora of different leadership styles that are proffered to the layman. Much like the issue of leadership definitions, every leadership "guru" also seems to have his own leadership style or method, which makes for a wide variety of opinions concerning which method is best and which leadership style should be used. And all these opinions must be sorted through in order to separate the wheat from the chaff. In this volume, however, I have endeavored to accomplish this task for you, minimizing the number of leadership styles that we will look at, as well as combining and merging a wide variety of different leadership approaches into only one or two comprehensive methods. Yet before we can move to examine these key leadership styles, it is necessary to address the issue of what a leadership style actually is, and how it is best defined.

Quite simply, what is meant by a leadership style is the conscious selection, by the leader, of a specific type of mode or approach used to deal with different leadership situations and circumstances, within the framework of the ten leadership principles and our definition of Catholic leadership. So while all the leadership principles are to be applied to every leadership situation in a *general* sense, it is the leader's leadership style that determines the details of *how, why, when, where, to whom, to what*, and *to what extent* those principles are to be applied in a specific leadership scenario. A leadership style deals with how we should adapt, modify, shift, enhance, or augment our general leadership principles given the circumstances of a particular leadership situation. And in understanding the idea of a leadership style in this initial manner, it is also possible to understand how it is distinctly different from the leadership principles themselves.

Yet in order to properly comprehend the difference between the leadership principles and a leadership style—a difference that needs to be truly appreciated before we can proceed to examine the actual leadership styles themselves—it is, furthermore, necessary to realize that the leadership principles are ultimately subsumed under the leadership style, and thus the leadership principles can be modified and adapted depending on the type of leadership style being used. For instance, consider just one part of the first leadership principle: Leading by example. In certain circumstances, such as when dealing with inexperienced subordinates or when involved in situations where your followers are near-paralyzed with fear, it may be necessary not only to lead from the front and by example, but also to do so in an extremely bold, overt, vocal, aggressive, flamboyant, and ultra-motivating fashion, thus providing a specific style of leadership by example that would motivate both inexperienced and fearful soldiers. By contrast, consider dealing with highly experienced or self-motivated subordinates. Leading from the front and by example for such people would consist of maintaining a silent but visible perseverance and fortitude, working later and longer than those same subordinates as well as providing quiet and subtle direction to those followers, which would convey a respect for their experience and knowledge, thus providing an overall style of non-boisterous leadership by example that would be the most effective in dealing with such individuals. In fact, given the situations described in both of these previous examples, it should be realized that if the hypothetical leader in those examples had used a leadership style diametrically opposed to the one that I recommended, then such a style of action would very likely have resulted in a catastrophic leadership failure. Indeed, just think how much the experienced subordinates of the latter example would have "appreciated" the strident and micro-managing style of leadership found in the former one. So it is clear that only certain styles of leadership are appropriate to certain situations as well as being appropriate to the overall conditions found in those situations. Furthermore, through the appreciation of these examples as well as others that could easily be imagined, it is made clear just how the leadership principles themselves stand firm and eternal in a general sense, regardless of what specific leadership style is being used, but simultaneously, it shows how these principles are adjusted and modified in their specific application *depending on* which leadership style is adopted. Both elements are thus unavoidably interdependent when practically applied.

Now, before exploring the idea of specifically Catholic leadership styles, it is profitable to gain a general knowledge of other leadership approaches that have been proposed and practiced by many different leaders. For example, one of the most commonly employed leadership styles, even if it is not being consciously used, is the Authoritarian leadership approach. Such a leadership style encourages the clear, direct, and overt use of a leader's organizational authority and command power. It stresses, in essence, the use of a leader's clout and ability to inflict punishment as central, while ultimately leading through fear and intimidation. Different from the Authoritarian style of leadership is the Participative method. This approach stresses the idea that subordinates should be intimately involved in the leadership process as well as having the leader focus on and seriously consider his subordinates' wishes and desires before making any leadership decision. Similar to this latter approach, the Democratic style of leadership goes even further, for it makes the leadership process a democratic endeavor in which leadership decisions are made by all members of the group, and with all members having equal input into the decision. The Coaching style of leadership focuses on the training and development of subordinates, helping them to find their own path and their own vision. By contrast, the Visionary approach to leadership has the leader boldly lay out the path for all to follow, while simultaneously setting the most innovative and unorthodox of leadership goals for the entire group. The Transformational style does precisely what it says: it seeks to lead in a manner that transforms an organization from an undesired form to a new, improved, and transformed structure. The Transitional style, by contrast, seeks only to lead in a manner that aids a group to survive major organizational transitions, such as when a business restructures and revamps its entire product line to something new and foreign, so this style is mainly focused on the management of the group during such a transition. The Management approach to leadership is one that avoids providing vision and direction, and sets these latter tasks to a lower priority than simply maintaining the organization that is being led; this style's leadership goal is, in essence, to maintain the group, not to develop it. Finally, the Free-Rein or Laissez-Faire style of leadership seeks to remove any overt or over-arching direction from the group's leader, and it focuses on allowing subordinates to make their own leadership decisions and to forge their own paths.

Though this list of leadership styles is in no way comprehensive, and even though an entire book could itself be written on each of these styles of leadership—and, indeed, entire books have been written about them—the point here is not to provide a full articulation of the concepts behind each of these leadership approaches, but rather to give a taste of the leadership flavor that each of them represent. For even by just having a taste of them, we can understand that from a Catholic leadership perspective, none of these leadership styles is satisfactory. And they are unsatisfactory not because the ideas behind them are not applicable to the Catholic leader, but rather because they do not employ the Catholic thoughts, concepts, and philosophy necessary to make the leadership style actually a *Catholic* one. Therefore, in order to create Catholic leaders, it is necessary to develop styles of leadership that are as Catholic as possible, both in their appearance and in their substance.

It should be noted, however, that we are not attempting to generate new leadership styles or approaches, as I earlier accused certain leadership experts or "gurus" of constantly doing. Rather, we are simply taking the most popular and most accepted leadership styles, summarizing them, and then placing them into a Catholic framework. Consequently, while the Catholic leadership styles soon to be presented may appear novel and unique, they are ultimately just Catholic reformulations and modifications of already accepted, functional, and effective secular leadership ideas. As such, within the Catholic leadership styles, you will find the very best of secular leadership knowledge combined with the vitally illuminating aspects of our Catholic faith, thus creating an unbeatable combination from which to generate our various approaches to leadership. In this manner, you will get the very best of both worlds, and your leadership will be the better for it.

The Catholic leadership styles

At their core, and when pared down to their most fundamental form, the styles of leadership apt and appropriate for a Catholic leader are necessarily linked to two elements that all Catholics will agree are utterly required of any Christian: love and faith. What this means in terms of leadership is that, from these two critical Christian ideas, two Catholic leadership styles naturally emerge. *Loving* leadership is the first style, which is characterized by active strength and dynamic leadership action. *Faithful* leadership is the second style, which is focused on exuding understanding, trust, confidence, and loyalty. It is, therefore, these two Catholic leadership styles—which will be shown to be more comprehensive then they may initially appear—that will be expanded on in the next two chapters.

A point of note, however, is in order before the next chapters are tackled. While in this book we will clearly delineate between these two rivaling Catholic leadership styles, it must be remembered that in practice, both of these leadership approaches meld into one another. In addition, while one style will be more appropriate to a given situation, just a moment later, as the leadership situation suddenly changes, the other Catholic leadership style may need to be adopted and put into practice. For that reason, it must be understood that while we are only exploring two styles of leadership, what is really being presented are *three* leadership methods, for even as the two clearly distinct styles are being overtly articulated in the coming pages, a third Catholic leadership approach is being implicitly presented, and it is a leadership approach that is created via a combination of the other two styles. Think, therefore, of Catholic leadership as a continuous spectrum, with both distinct styles of leadership at each end of that spectrum, and with a great deal of middle ground that naturally generates a third leadership approach. And this third Catholic leadership style is one that allows for a great deal of adaptation, flexibility, and situational accommodation.

With these important facts now made clear and plain, let us seek out and explore the two foundational styles of Catholic leadership that every member of the Faith *needs* to put into practice.

CHAPTER 15
THE ACTIVE STRENGTH OF LOVE

A WHOLE PLATOON of new soldiers: thirty-five pairs of eyes looking at me expectantly, each one waiting for something, each one waiting to hear some novel idea or a unique word of wisdom. They were all fresh off the bus, so to speak, and so new that they were like newborn babies, unable to care for themselves even if they tried. And they were now all expecting me to show them the way. Not that I was any great or experienced military officer at this point in time, but that ultimately did not matter, for they were all still expecting me to lead them. Indeed, having only a few years of experience myself, I had just been sent down to a military training facility to instruct and teach these brand new recruits, and they did not care that I was almost as young and as "green" as they were. I was their leader, and they expected me to act as such. There was, furthermore, no doubt that I would, as obviously required by my rank and position. And although I only had a few years of military experience, they were years of the most intense and direct learning, and they thus distinguished me in high degree from these utterly new soldiers—just as in two to three years these currently new soldiers would be utterly different in skill and knowledge from brand new recruits. Yet it was daunting, as can be imagined, to think that I would have to lead and direct men and women totally dependent on me for all their initial skill, knowledge, and future military ability. How could this be done? And more importantly, how could it be done well? What leadership style could I employ in such a vital leadership situation? What leadership approach would be best suited to such a circumstance?

The answer to all these questions, from the Catholic leadership perspective, is *love*. Indeed, the method of leadership that we must utilize in such circumstances is a leadership style filled with an active, strong, and enduring love.

It must be immediately understood that we are not speaking of love in the modern sense, the sense that seems to equate love with mere sentimentality, infatuation, or other powerful but similarly unreasoned "feelings," thereby simplifying and degrading it. In fact, this modern and common cultural understanding of love is but one of the reasons for the difficulty in seeing Jesus as a figure of total love, for the love that Jesus embodies and pours out for all is of a different kind and quality than is accepted in today's individualistic and permissive society. Jesus gives us true love. He provides us with a love that encompasses the emotional and the sentimental, but is not bound by them. It is a love that stems from the heart and the head, thus allowing the head to support the heart when the latter falters in its duties, while at the same time permitting the heart to warm the head when it becomes too cold and calculating. It is a love that stems from *all* the human faculties: emotion and instinct as well as the intellect and the will. And thus just as God the Father Himself does, Jesus gives all of humanity the love of a *parent*—a term that has also lost much of its true and traditional meaning in popular culture—and it is from understanding this type of love that we can ultimately understand the leadership style of love.

Beyond employing all human faculties, the love of a parent is a love that wishes the very best for the person being loved, regardless of what that means for the feelings, pride, emotion, or psychology of the loved person. Such a love is kind if kindness is what is best. Such a love disciplines if discipline is what is required. Such a love is patient if patience is what is ideal given the situation. And such a love is direct, forceful, commanding, and authoritarian if necessary. Ultimately, such a love is whatever it needs to be—in keeping, of course, with the first portion of the Catholic definition of leadership—in order to do what is truly in the best interests of the person being loved. From all this, it is possible to recognize that such a love will not be afraid of "hurting" another individual's feelings if that is what is required, or shattering an individual's false ego if that is what is best, or taking over the control and direction of a situation if that is what is needed to provide ideal leadership in that specific circumstance. And most of all, such a love is not only active, but clearly *pro-active;* it seeks out ways in which to show itself and employ itself for the betterment of those loved. Thus, all these aspects of true love need to be understood, for it is only with such an understanding of love firmly held and fully grasped that it is possible to proceed into the details of this leadership style.

When we love, we obviously love others and not just ourselves, for love is ultimately something that must be directed at others in order to be true. Realizing this fact, we ask the question: With whom are we to employ a leadership style of Catholic love?

The answer stems directly from our understanding of love, for if love is a pro-active force that seeks the best interests of the people being loved, then this suggests that those particular individuals are not necessarily capable of doing what is best for their own selves, so they need an active force to assist them. And this would indeed be the active force of love, which the Catholic leader must employ if he is to achieve what is best for all the people under his charge. Now, by understanding all these ideas, it is possible to see that such a style of Catholic leadership is specifically and primarily to be used when dealing with certain kinds of subordinates: the inexperienced, the untrained, the unskilled, the stressed, the uncertain, and the confused. All of these types of followers share the common feature of needing loving direction and guidance.

The inexperienced, so often being men and women of the very young variety, need firm direction and clear guidance in all aspects of life, and thus the leader has an even greater task to accomplish in such cases. The untrained may have certain life experiences under their belt, but have none of the specific training that will be required of them in their new position, and thus need loving leadership to provide them with that training and instruction. The unskilled may have both experience and training, but are currently poor at what they do, and thus need a loving leader to provide them with support, supervision, and patience. The stressed subordinate may have both training and skill, but lacks the ability to operate properly in certain high-intensity situations, thus necessitating a leader to provide him with clear command and control. The uncertain follower may be encountering a new and foreign situation for the first time, and due to being unsure of what to do, he looks to the leader for his sense of direction and proper conduct. And finally, the confused may, for whatever reason, be as experienced as possible but simply not understand the goal of a particular task, and thus need the leadership of a loving leader to enlighten his confusion and lead the way. So these are all the types of subordinates for whom the loving style of leadership is ideally suited. And having now articulated these ideas, we can move forward and examine *when* employing loving leadership is most appropriate.

Just as the existence of inexperienced, untrained, or highly stressed soldiers requires a commander to use a form of loving leadership to deal with them, situations that are highly stressful, novel, uncertain, extremely dangerous, time constrained, or confusing also require such a leadership style. Subordinates in highly stressful situations may become flustered and under-perform, thus needing a higher level of guidance and control than they would normally require, as well as needing a leader to be lovingly pro-active in such situations. New, novel, and unique situations may catch even the most seasoned individual off guard, leaving him unsure of himself and paralyzed with indecision, thereby forcing the leader to provide swift direction and command. Uncertain circumstances may render subordinates unable to make decisions on their own, even decisions that they would easily make under normal circumstances, meaning that a leader must lovingly step in to take the reins in such situations and thus relieve his subordinates of their uncertainty. Similar to the last example, extremely dangerous and violent events often leave men and women understandably frozen with fear, and thus the leader must overcome such situational fear with his love. Situations that are time constrained simply do not provide the time necessary to permit subordinates to determine different ways to deal with the state of affairs on their own, and so such situations require a loving leader to immediately and directly guide the group in the achievement of its aims. And situations that are mired in confusion and miscommunication, where disorder abounds, need a loving leader to cut straight through such mire and transform this disorder and miscommunication into order and clarity. Therefore, it is clear that the Catholic style of loving leadership is a style that is best suited to situations of intense pressure, high tension, and heavy trauma, where the leader must stand at the proverbial front of his subordinates with his banner held high and the words "Follow Me" on his lips, while charging forward towards the enemy.

These visualizations of when love is best employed as a leadership style, as well as with whom it is ideally employed, provide an excellent means of understanding love as a leadership style. Yet it is also beneficial to see if it is possible to explain *how else* we can perceive the Catholic style of loving leadership, and what other terms are subsumed and integrated into this particular leadership style. For example, we can see how certain other leadership terms form, after a manner, the background to the love style of leadership. And such other terms might include the following: Vision Provider, Decision Maker, Disciplinarian, Authoritarian, Controller, Commander, Leader, Chief, Ruler, Boss, Teacher, Tutor, Coach, Lecturer, and Instructor. The terms Vision Provider and Decision Maker show us that a loving leader supplies goals, aims, and direction for the group, and makes decisions for the group in order to achieve those goals and aims. The terms Disciplinarian, Authoritarian, and Controller show us how a loving leader must, at times, discipline the group for transgressions, control the group as required to maintain direction, and be authoritarian in his power and authority if necessitated by the leadership circumstances. The terms Commander, Leader, Chief, Ruler, and Boss demonstrate that a loving leader must also understand and remember that he is indeed a leader, who must command, rule, and even boss his subordinates as required in order to achieve the group's aims and goals. And the terms Teacher, Tutor, Coach, Lecturer, and Instructor provide a means of seeing that a loving leader must promote the continuous training and teaching of his subordinates in all the skills required for their future success. All these sub-terms, which are subsumed and which support the overall style of loving leadership, demonstrate that such leadership is unavoidably active and dynamic. It is a type of leadership where the leader's love seeks to show itself as well as express itself fully and vigorously.

We have thus examined this topic of loving leadership from a general and practical perspective. But since we are primarily examining this issue as Catholics, it is also necessary to study it from a more Christian-focused and scriptural point of view. And in order to achieve this deeper Christian understanding of what loving leadership should be, there is no better individual to turn to than Saint Paul. For in his first letter to the Corinthians, the Apostle Paul writes a passage about love that is as sublime as it is meaningful:

> Love is patient, love is kind. It does not envy, it does not boast, it is not proud. It is not rude, it is not self-seeking, it is not easily angered, it keeps no record of wrongs. Love does not delight in evil but rejoices with the truth. It always protects, always trusts, always hopes, always perseveres. Love never fails (1 Corinthians 13:4-8, NIV).

There is arguably no summary of love that is as simultaneously beautiful and comprehensive as this one is. It is the deepest form of poetry and verse. Yet even more importantly, this passage is also immensely instructive, for it provides us with a key template from which to understand what love is, and therefore to understand what we need *to be* if we are to be loving Catholic leaders. In light of this fact, and in order to solidify our grasp of love as a leadership tool, it is thus to our great benefit to thoroughly examine and carefully elucidate each of the elements articulated by Saint Paul.

Love is patient
This fact should be fairly self-evident, for when the needs of the types of individuals that call for the loving style of

leadership are reflected upon, it becomes clear that patience is an indispensible leadership attribute. A teacher or a coach cannot be successful if he is not patient, for it is through patience, and the additional time that patience brings with it, that a subordinate's skills, abilities, and talents are developed to their greatest degree.

Love is kind
Much like the first trait, the loving leader must be kind to those he leads for the very same reasons that he must be patient with them. Indeed, the types of subordinates that call for the loving style of leadership require such kindness. Yet we must not understand this kindness as all pervasive, for it must be tempered by the other elements of love, as we will soon discover.

Love does not envy
If you are a leader who truly seeks to love the subordinates that you lead, how can you be envious of them, for envy breeds both dislike from you and distrust from them? In contrast to this selfishness, the loving leader should be both happy and joyful of that which his subordinates have, but which he does not possess. And he should be joyful for them not only because such a joy naturally comes from love, but also because as the leader of the group, he already partakes, after a certain manner, in all that his subordinates have. Truly, as a Catholic leader, your subordinates' happiness should be *your* happiness, and thus you should possess no reason to be envious of them.

Love does not boast
There is an old military adage that as a leader, all your team's successes, *even though* led by you, belong to them. And by

contrast, all your team's failures, *because* they are ultimately led by you, belong to you and you alone. And though not a universally applicable saying, it is one which should be adopted by any Catholic leader practicing loving leadership. Consequently, by adopting this leadership truism, you thereby lose all room to boost, for no success actually belongs to you. You cannot boast of that which you are not taking credit for! Furthermore, let it never be forgotten that as a leader, your primary aim is to achieve your mission via effective leadership, not to boast about doing so.

Love is not proud
What has been said about boasting is equally applicable here, yet there is also a further, specifically Christian point to make concerning being proud: pride goes before the Fall! Indeed, of all the sins that mankind may fall prey to, pride is the deadliest. And this fact is not only true for a Catholic leader, but it is actually *magnified* for him. For there are few things that naturally hold the potential to make you exceedingly proud than the authority and power innate in leadership, and yet there are simultaneously few things that will make your subordinates come to despise you more than a *false* sense of pride. And no orthodox Catholic, knowing what he does about mankind and about what the Church teaches, should believe himself justified or capable of possessing a true and good sense of pride. Furthermore, since the Catholic believer knows that all good things within him are ultimately from God, then such a faithful Catholic should readily embrace the warranted confidence in himself that does come from God the Father, but should spurn the pride that does not.

Love is not rude
Love is honest, not rude. This truth, however, must not be misunderstood, for while honesty may be *perceived* as rude by

those receiving the honesty, this perception is ultimately unimportant. Indeed, because of the fact that what is perceived by another individual cannot be controlled by you, it is therefore beside the point and should be disregarded. What can be controlled is truthfulness and honesty, two traits that must always be total and not submit to rudeness, vileness, or even cowardice.

Love is not self-seeking
A self-seeking Catholic is an oxymoron, for a Catholic is always to seek God's will, not his own; and a Catholic leader must also seek out and promote the personal good of his subordinates above any of his own needs, regardless of the situation or circumstance. There is, therefore, not even an inch of room for self-seeking behaviour in a Catholic leader who is aiming to lead with love and compassion. It is simply not possible.

Love is not easily angered
Again, based on the fact that a Catholic leader employing the loving style of leadership is primarily dealing with inexperienced, unskilled, or uncertain subordinates, it is necessary for him to be slow to anger—which links back to the trait of patience that has already been discussed. But let it be noticed that this in no way excludes justifiable and warranted anger, for indeed such anger is fully available to the Catholic leader. Such anger aids with discipline, correction, and control, and is thus indispensible to the loving leader, even if it is to be used most sparingly.

Love keeps no record of wrongs
Confusion cannot be allowed to enter here, and therefore the Catholic underpinnings of this particular element of love must

immediately be brought forth. For under the Catholic interpretation of this passage, love indeed keeps no record of wrongs *as long as* repentance for those wrongs is provided, confessed, and accepted. And such an interpretation is precisely the one that should be adopted by a loving leader, for such a leader must ensure that his subordinates first admit and confess their wrong-doings, then immediately seek to rectify any of these wrongs. It is only within this context that wrongs are not recorded, and it is only in this manner that this particular element of love should be employed.

Love does not delight in evil
Quite simply, how can a Catholic, let alone a loving Catholic leader, delight in evil? He cannot, and the matter is as simple as this.

Love rejoices with the truth
As with the point above, how can a Catholic leader *not* rejoice in the truth—the truth which is Catholicism and Catholic leadership—that he holds? He cannot *but* rejoice, and again as above, the matter is truly as simple as that.

Love always protects
Like a mother (or father) who protects her children from as much harm as she is able to, so must a loving leader, to the best of his abilities, strive to protect those individuals that he leads. Yet it must be remembered that protection does not necessarily equate to total sheltering. Indeed, it will at times be necessary to permit controlled and mitigated harm, suffering, and pain to come to those that you lead in order to provide them, by teaching them to protect themselves, with better protection and more comprehensive security in the future. Thus protection includes both a sheltering of your

subordinates, as well as a selective allowance for those same subordinates to leave your sheltering wing and learn the dangers and hardships of reality for themselves.

Love always trusts
Although fully endorsed as a necessary part of loving leadership, this is a point that is best articulated in the subsequent chapter on faithful leadership. What can be said here, however, is that the fact that love always trusts intimately connects the loving style of leadership with the leadership style of faithfulness. And trust is thus the very virtue that ultimately creates the continuum of leadership which exists between these two different approaches to leading men and women.

Love always hopes
Even in the jaws of death and defeat, when all reasons for optimism seem lost, the loving leader always holds on to hope. For if the leader himself falters in this task, then how can those he leads hold on to any hope? Indeed, when everything seems lost, then the loving Catholic leader—as a Catholic and follower of Christ—must stand firm regardless of the hope, or lack thereof, which those around him have. And a Catholic leader like you should always realize and remember that love holds on to hope, because it always holds on to Christ. So never lose hope!

Love always perseveres
We have made it abundantly clear that the loving Catholic leader is to set a vision and a goal for those that he leads, but what must also be clear is that the loving Catholic leader simultaneously needs to persevere in seeking and striving towards those goals. Thus, the Catholic leader, displaying his

love, must also display his perseverance and fortitude in holding fast to the group's vision and goals, no matter what may occur to those around him when he does so.

Love never fails

Now, considering the frailty and fallibility of human beings, the claim that *love never fails* may seem quite difficult to believe, but from a leadership perspective it is both true as well as being an excellent point to end this section on. For while it is obviously the case that a leader's love for his subordinates will falter and thus fail them at times, what it will not do is fail you as a leader! But what does this mean? It means that if, as a Catholic leader, you always *strive* to love those that follow you, then they will still respect and cherish you as a leader, even though your love may waver from time to time. And I can attest to this truth from my own leadership experience, for though I made more than my fair share of mistakes throughout my military career, I also strove to always love my soldiers, and they truly did not hold those numerous mistakes against me—a fact that they told me of themselves. So beyond a shadow of a doubt, love as a leadership style will not fail you as a leader, even though you will fail it more times than you should.

In closing, it is necessary, as it always is, to return to the *living* example of Catholic leadership: Jesus Christ. And thus the question of whether Jesus Christ is an example of a loving leader must therefore be raised. Yet it is almost a pointless question, for not only is Christ indeed an example of a loving leader, He is perhaps the only *true* example of a loving leader. For Jesus Christ, as God-made-man, is simultaneously Love-made-man; He is true and full love, which is a level of love that quite simply cannot be fully realized by any human leader. And as Christ is not only the leader of the Church, but also of all creation, then Christ truly is, in the most vital sense, the one true and complete loving leader to have ever walked this earth. From Him, all loving leadership comes, and to us He not only provides such leadership in its totality but also demonstrates it in its fullness. In view of this fact, perhaps the more important question thus becomes whether or not we see any of the ideas discussed in this section within Jesus' earthly ministry?

Again, it takes but a few moments of reading any one of the Gospels—just one, not even all four—to see that Jesus Christ, when He began His preaching, came on the scene with an unprecedented vision and purpose. Jesus not only provided His closest disciples with specific goals, but also with the direction necessary to seek out and achieve those goals. And even with the general populace that He preached to, Jesus acted as a teacher, coach, and instructor, not only through His words but also with His actions. Christ, furthermore, exemplified Saint Paul's description of love. This, of course, is in no way surprising, as Saint Paul is taking his cues from Christ Himself. Indeed, Jesus was both patient and kind. He was not envious, even when tempted by the devil with all the worldly goods that He could not have. Christ never boasted, but plainly and directly stated who He was and what He had to do. And Christ was not rude, but honest. Christ, moreover, never sought His own will, but always sought the will of His Father in Heaven. Christ also angered slowly, only once showing His physical wrath against the money-changers in the temple. Jesus Christ, furthermore, upon receiving the repentance of many, equally forgave those many, keeping no record of their wrongs. And being both sinless and truth itself, Christ showed no delight in evil, but always promoted the joy that truth naturally brings. Finally Christ, even though it led to His own death, always protected His flock, always trusted His

Father, and always had hope in His Father, thereby persevering to the very end. So Christ never failed and His love never failed; Christ is, therefore, truly the epitome of loving leadership.

CHAPTER 16
THE PASSIVE POWER OF FAITH

AS FAR AS leadership situations go, it was the utter opposite of when I was training the brand new recruits at the start of their budding military careers—as described at the beginning of the last chapter. For this time, I was the new one; I was the unproven and untested officer striving to take over and lead an experienced platoon of over thirty hardened infantry soldiers, each of whom had just returned from a tour overseas in a combat zone. You can talk about work stress, but you have likely never experienced the particular form of pressure and anxiety that can weigh on you when the eyes of thirty trained and capable soldiers are watching your every move with both eagerness and anticipation, each of them just waiting to see what you will do or how you will react. Such was the leadership situation that I found myself in when I first arrived, fresh from the completion of my own training, to fulfill the requirements of my new career. And, humorously enough, this type of situation and circumstance not only happened to me once, but twice, with the second time being even more severe. For when I transferred from the Infantry trade to the Intelligence profession, I suddenly found myself thrust into yet another situation where I was the "new" soldier—even with my previous military experience. Once again I had to start from scratch in terms of adapting my leadership style and methodology to suit this new situation and the new methods of operating within the Intelligence field. There was, furthermore, the interesting fact that all the Intelligence soldiers under me were specialists within their respective sub-fields, having skills and knowledge that were foreign to me, and as such, in nearly all of my interactions with them, I was not only new, but also unskilled. I may have had the leadership skills to lead these men and women in general military duties, but at the start of my new career as an Intelligence Officer, I most definitely did not have the leadership skills and ideas required to lead them properly in this specialist trade. So the inevitable and necessary question arose: How, in either of these situations, was I to lead these soldiers? What leadership style was I to employ? What type of leader should I become? And most importantly, given my Catholicism, what would a Catholic leader do in such a situation?

To respond to these four questions with an answer that should be in no way foreign to any Catholic, we must turn to the idea of faith. It is faith that answers these questions, and it is indeed a leadership style centered on faith that provides the key to leading in such circumstances. A faithful leadership style is thus the opposite of dynamic love, and being so, it is naturally the one that should be used in situations where active love is inappropriate.

Just as with love, however, it is also necessary to be absolutely clear on what *faith* means in this context, for it is a term that is greatly misunderstood by many people who do not possess it, and even by some who do. Faith, unlike the modern caricature of it, is not an idea, attitude, or state of being that is adopted due to a lack of evidence in something. Rather, faith is a trust that is held and maintained in something for which there exists a preponderance of evidence, yet not utter certainty. Faith is a bridge that allows our belief in something to rationally move from a reasonable belief in it due to the evidence for it, to an existential certainty about it. So, for example, the Catholic may have a great number of reasons for being Catholic, and he may be eminently rational and reasonable for holding Catholicism as true, but he does not necessarily have absolute and utter certainty of Catholicism's truth. This is where faith enters and provides him with that certainty, so that he can hold to Catholicism as the *fullness of truth* in his daily life. As stated earlier, faith is trust; it means having the evidence necessary to take the final step forward in any decision or course of action. It is the trust in something or someone for which you have enough evidence and knowledge to warrant trusting unto certainty.

Adding to this idea of faith as a form of trust is the author of the Book of Hebrews, who states: "Now faith is the assurance of things hoped for, the conviction of things not seen" (Hebrews 11:1, ESV). So from this scriptural quotation, we are shown that not only does faith mean trust, but it is also linked to the idea of hope, and of having the assurance and conviction that our hope and trust will be fulfilled. With this dual understanding of the nature of faith now explained, it is possible to begin formulating our knowledge of how to *lead* by faith.

If faith means both hope and trust, and if it is to be used as a leadership style, then it must naturally be seen as a style of leadership that is most effective when applied to subordinates that are highly skilled, vastly knowledgeable, and greatly experienced. It is a style applicable to the leadership of veterans, for it would be such experienced followers who would provide the evidence necessary to show that they can be trusted, and in whom hope could be placed for the assured completion of any assigned task or project. Think, for example, of whom you would trust with a major and critical mission that your organization needed effectively and efficiently accomplished? Naturally, you would not place such a task in the hands of a novice subordinate, but rather in the hands of your most experienced follower. I know from my own military background that I always ensured that my most important tasks were assigned to my best and most experienced men, those I could trust with the task asked of them. It is a reliance on the skill and experience of your subordinates, especially when you are lacking such skill and experience yourself—as I was in the various examples given at the start of this chapter—that marks the faithful style of leadership.

Now, even though a Catholic leader could apply this faith-based style of leadership to any given situation, its effectiveness being dependent on the strength and expertise of the subordinates that he has in those situations, it is simultaneously the case that this particular leadership style is better suited to certain situations than to others. Situations of low stress and circumstances with large amounts of time, as well as conditions that provide ample opportunity for consultation with other individuals, all provide the best circumstances in which to employ the faith-based leadership style. For in such situations trust and hope are allowed to grow, build, and develop in a manner that then generates even greater trust and hope. Again, this is not to say that such a leadership style cannot be used in other, more intense leadership circumstances, but rather that it is not as preferable in such situations as a loving style of leadership would be. Yet what is most peculiar is that this faithful style of leadership is needed, at times, in the very situations that you would not imagine it to be. Picture the most intense combat scene, with bullets flying and soldiers screaming. Such a situation requires direct and engaging leadership, yet it also requires trust in your sub-commanders and sub-leaders, as well as the hope that they will carry out the orders that you have assigned to them. So it is possible to see how this faith-based leadership is more widely applicable and more useful than might normally be imagined.

To fully understand and appreciate these ideas concerning the fusion of faith and leadership, it is also most instructive to provide various comparisons with these concepts. As such, in secular terms, we can understand the faithful style of leadership in a number of different ways. The first way is through the acknowledgement that faith stands for freedom. This means that the Catholic leader practicing this style of leadership grants his subordinates great freedom and latitude to make their own choices based on their experiences and their own expertise. It is also a style of leadership that is "laid-back" and allows for self-determination. Such a leadership approach encourages the development of a subordinate's own leadership abilities and skill, while additionally demonstrating a leader's trust in his subordinates due to his willingness to allow for such self-determination. Most certainly, a faithful leader is a trusting leader, and as such he permits such freedom and self-determination through the adoption of a more permissive attitude—not in the sense of being morally permissive, but permissive in the sense of allowing subordinates to make their own decisions within a correct moral framework—which serves to illustrate his trust. In a certain manner, this is a passive style of leadership, a style that does not desire to firmly take charge of a situation, nor one that wishes to immediately assert its authority or command. In line with this, the faithful Catholic leader is one who, in the making of his leadership decisions, allows his subordinates and followers to participate and make their own opinions known to him. By allowing the views of others to strongly shape the leader's ultimate decision in a given situation, it is a leadership style that is democratic in flavor. This is why this faith-focused leadership style is most suitable in situations with ample decision-making time and low stress, for it is primarily in such situations that a democratic decision-making process can take place. Furthermore, the fact that faithful leadership is the style best suited to a participative decision-making process is at the same time the reason why it is the best leadership style to use with highly experienced and knowledgeable subordinates, for such subordinates can be trusted to provide sound and objective opinions when engaged in democratic decision making.

We must also appreciate the fact that a faithful leader is a mentor and a counselor. A mentor does indeed provide his subordinates with advice and a living example to emulate, but his primary goal is to have those subordinates develop their own skills and experience. So a mentor may assist his followers by providing them with a general framework within which they can work, but the mentor does not provide the specific details of how or when this work must be done. Those items are left to the subordinates to decide. In the same manner, the Catholic who is a faithful leader acts as a counselor to his subordinates. And a counselor does precisely what his title implies: he counsels, advocates, and recommends.

Now, in contrast to the leadership style of an active love, which we can understand as strongly *pulling* subordinates towards a specific goal or aim, the leadership style of a passive faith gently *pushes* subordinates towards a goal or aim. Whereas loving leadership leads, implying that the leader is to be at the front of his group having them follow him, faithful leadership directs, implying that the leader is to be at the back of his group having them find their own way to the desired objective, but is also always ready to correct the group and assist them if they stray too far off course. In sum, the loving leader provides his inexperienced and uncertain subordinates with an objective to capture, but is also intimately involved during every step of the process in order to see that objective achieved. The faithful leader also provides his experienced and certain subordinates with an objective, but he trusts them to achieve that objective without the need for his own detailed interference. The faithful leader essentially says to his followers: "Due to your knowledge, experience, and expertise, I trust you to get the job done without my direct oversight or intervention, so get it done!"

Yet being a faithful leader means not only placing trust in your subordinates, but in your superiors as well. The faithful Catholic leader understands that there obviously exist many superiors deserving of both respect and trust. And towards such superiors a faithful style of leadership must be applied, for such leaders have earned the trust and hope that can be placed in them. It is granted, of course, that certain superiors do not meet such a criterion, and in such cases, a loving style of leadership is the more appropriate means of dealing with them. So, all told, it must be remembered that the faithful approach to leadership is suitable both as a style that can assist a leader whether he is looking upwards at his superiors or downwards at his subordinates. And even in the life of Christ we see a foremost example of faithful leadership, whether it is looking upwards or downwards.

When He is following, listening, and trusting God the Father, we can see in Christ the deepest faith. Trusting the Father unto death, Christ has the conviction and the hope to hold to the Father's mission till the very end, and in so doing, He achieves the mission that both He and the Father desired. Christ's words and actions reveal an individual *fully* trusting in the will of His own leader, who in this case is God the Father. Now, this is not to say that we, as solely human leaders, should put such *full* faith in either our human superiors or our human subordinates, but rather that strong faith in someone for whom such a faith is warranted is not only a leadership virtue, but is exemplified by Jesus Christ and should thus be practiced. Furthermore, it is possible to see how Christ Himself praises and lauds such individuals as the faithful Centurion who, recognizing Jesus Christ as Master and Lord, has such a faith in Christ that he knows that whatever he asks can indeed be done by Jesus. This Centurion, though a very powerful leader, knew when to humble himself and when to trust in the leadership and power of an even greater leader: Jesus Christ.

The Gospels also provide us with many counter examples to both of these positive illustrations, for Christ is often admonishing His followers for their lack of faith in Him. It is Peter's lack of faith that causes him to sink into the stormy waters after walking on them, even though Christ is immediately beside him and fully supporting him with His power (Matthew 14:25-33). And it is their lack of faith in Jesus Christ and His power that so often leads Christ to have to remind His followers of His mission, His mandate, and His divine authority.

We have thus seen that for an orthodox Catholic, a faithful style of leadership is highly useful for a variety of situations. It is crucial for the leader when he himself is inexperienced or uncertain of his new surroundings and must therefore trust those subordinates that are experienced and certain. It is also crucial for the leader to employ when dealing with trustworthy and experienced superiors as well as trustworthy and experienced subordinates. And it is crucial for the leader to use when a situation calls for participative and democratic leadership.

CATHOLIC LEADERSHIP

The Catholic leader thus has at his disposal an overall leadership methodology that can utilize either active love, passive faith, or a combination of the two in order to create ingenious and adaptive leadership styles suitable for all situations. For between these three approaches to leadership, it is feasible to succeed in any leadership situation or circumstance. It is, in essence, entirely possible to become a strong, capable, and Christ-like Catholic leader.

CHAPTER 17
ARE YOU A CATHOLIC LEADER?

TEN YEARS. Ten *hard* years. Ten hard years of extremely rewarding service in an outstanding organization, with the unrepeatable experience of having led some of the best men and women in the world. This was the thought that ran through my mind as I sat stunned in front of my new Commanding Officer, who had just surprised me beyond words. Indeed, the entire situation would have been downright comical if it had not been so unexpected and sudden; the scene was made even more astonishing given that I had just been assigned to this new military outfit, and that the conversation that I was having with my Commanding Officer was the very first one that we had ever had. And what he had said to me, which had so shocked me, was that I was finished. I was being released from the military. I was, essentially, being fired. Due to an ongoing medical condition—which I had previously been told would *not* affect my military status or career—I was informed that I would be removed from the very organization that I had spent over a decade devoting my life to. I would be released from the only life that I had known, and the very one that I had planned to see through to my eventual retirement.

To say that this was a sudden and extreme shock would be an understatement, although it is the type of shock that I am sure many people can imagine and also one that many people have probably experienced themselves. Nevertheless, and regardless of the shock, it did not take me long to compose myself, to adapt to these new circumstances, to overcome this sudden obstacle, and to make a decision about my new future. Indeed, though the release process would take up to six months, it took less than a day for me to gather my thoughts, formulate a plan, and prepare to move on, and my ability to do so stemmed not from any innate skill on my part, but was due in very large measure to the living application of the leadership skills and ideas articulated in this book. Yet as I did prepare to move on from the life that had guided all my adult years and my professional training, it was both predictable and unavoidable that I would reflect on the past decade. In particular, it was inevitable that I would think on my leadership, and on whether or not I had succeeded as a leader. Had I been a good leader? Had I been effective? Strong? Capable? Moral? Now, such questions, though hard to assess objectively and to quantify properly, naturally rear their head when a person who has been in a leadership role his entire career suddenly finishes with it. And of course, it was no different with me, especially since I had been asking myself those very same questions every day of every month of every year for my whole career. In fact, I had been asking myself such questions even before I joined the military.

Now, though a full, complete, and absolute answer to all these questions is ultimately elusive, such questions do raise an important and final issue that does warrant a comprehensive response: How do we know what makes for a successful leader? How do we know if *we* have been successful leaders? And what should we look for to gauge such leadership success?

This thought of how to gauge our success as leaders is an idea that is foundational and absolutely necessary to contemplate for any individual in a leadership role. Indeed, throughout this book, we have covered a vast number of different topics. But here, at this book's end, while contemplating how to gauge our success as leaders, it is necessary to turn full circle and to return to this book's beginning. Once there, we remember that we examined and defined the term *leadership*, showing it to be more than just mere authority or management, and articulating how it necessarily includes the shepherding and guidance of free people. More specifically, we explicitly defined *Catholic leadership*, which is a definition of such criticality and importance to our endeavor of gauging leadership success—due to the fact that within this definition, all the key themes of this book are summarized and condensed—that it is a definition worth repeating in full:

In keeping with the example of Christ, the teachings of the Catholic Church and absolute obedience to moral truth, Catholic leadership is both the art and the science of guiding, shepherding, and managing other free-willed persons towards created and sustained goals, aims, and an overall Catholic vision, without solely or explicitly relying on visible authority or coercive power—God willing.

As I mentioned in the first chapter of this volume, if nothing else is taken from this book, it should be this definition, for from it a great portion of what constitutes excellent Catholic leadership can already be gleaned and put into practice.

Beyond this definition, we also examined that, due to Jesus Christ's vast social influence and historical effect, He is not only a prime candidate to develop a leadership strategy from, but *the* prime candidate, with no other historical individuals rising above Jesus in terms of their overall leadership weight or effect. Furthermore, it was shown that developing a leadership strategy that combined both a military perspective as well as a Catholic one is in no way opposed either to Sacred Scripture or Church teachings. Once all these aspects were established, we then moved to the leadership principles themselves. First, we explained that all leaders must not only lead by example but must also always remember to actually lead, meaning that they must act as the group's primary decision maker and problem solver. Next, we examined how in order to be a successful leader, we must always remain aware of our circumstances, stay current with them, and gather intelligence, noting the difference between intelligence and simple information. It is better to give than to receive was the next principle that was articulated. For the fourth principle, it was argued that communicating clearly and keeping your team strategically informed is a key leadership idea. After this, we explained that you must always guide, teach, and train both your followers and yourself. We then moved to the principle that always showing interest, concern, and impartiality is crucial to leading others. Knowing and understanding when and how to be a follower, as opposed to always pushing for the leadership role, was explained next. Then it was, somewhat cryptically, shown that as a leader sometimes we must be more than a friend, less than a friend, and at times, just a friend, meaning that we must symbolically adopt the natural familial roles of mother, father, and sibling. Afterwards, we examined why a leader must always be ready to take a stand for what he believes in, and if necessary, why he must be ready to stand alone. Last, the principle of *becoming* the leadership principles, meaning living them fully and completely as a leader, was elucidated and reinforced. After studying these ten leadership principles, we summarized two key Catholic leadership strategies and styles. We examined how an active and strong love is the ideal method for leading inexperienced and uncertain subordinates, moving finally to the study of how a trusting faith is the best way of leading the experienced and certain. And thus, through this full examination of leadership from a specifically Catholic perspective, it truly is possible for any individual reading and applying the ideas found in this book to become an outstanding, respected, and trusted leader, regardless of his profession or position.

Yet the fact remains that even with all these ideas and concepts expressed and articulated, and even with all of them being put into practice by you, the essential question asked above still remains: How do we gauge our success as Catholic leaders? Indeed, as stated, this vital, necessary, and unavoidable question still waits for an answer. The issue of how we determine the success or failure of our leadership stares every Catholic leader in the face; in fact, it stares at all leaders, every single moment of every single day. And thus this question not only demands an answer, it screams for one.

So how can we answer this question? What precise means can we use to test the success or failure of our leadership skills, and more specifically, to test our leadership abilities as *Catholic* leaders? Whose views and opinions are to be used to assist us in this quest to determine our leadership capability? Whose advice should be sought?

Though it rightly appears that we have already been inundated with questions, it will likely not be surprising that the way to answer all these previous questions about how to measure our success as Catholic leaders comes, in fact, from other questions. And these *new* questions arise directly from our contemplation of what Catholic leadership is and what it means, thus bringing us, once again, back to the very definition from which we started. Indeed, we return directly to the definition of Catholic leadership, and the key parts that form that definition. For from these different parts stem all the new questions that are essential for a Catholic leader to ask himself in order to determine if he truly is a good, worthy, and honorable leader. These are, therefore, the very questions that every Catholic leader must ask himself, as well as the questions that every Catholic leader *must answer honestly* if he is to judge the true value of his Catholic leadership:

In keeping with the example of Christ...

- Do you strive to emulate Christ in all things, who is the example of perfection itself, and is thus necessarily the perfect example of Catholic leadership?
- Do you obey Jesus Christ and His commands in all things, thus holding fast to those things that will strengthen and reinforce your Catholic leadership, such as prayer, penance, and piety?
- Do you know and submit, every moment of every day, to the Lord Jesus Christ Himself, thus being guided and led yourself by the living Lord and greatest leader of all?

...the teachings of the Catholic Church

- Do you stand firm in the Faith and hold fast to the Truth, thus having a firm foundation and unwavering guide on which to plant the pillar of your own leadership?
- Do you profess your Catholicism in all things and in all aspects of your life, showing yourself to *be* Catholic without fear or fright, and thus truly being a *Catholic* leader?
- Do you know the teachings of the Church, such that you can lead others, whether Catholic or not, to the Truth that you hold?

...and absolute obedience to moral truth

- Do you obey your conscience and bind your will to moral truth, thus becoming not only a leader but a light for the world?
- Do you look yourself in the mirror daily with virtuous humility and motivating guilt, thus reminding yourself of the critical charge that you hold as a Catholic leader?
- Do you promote, understand, and live moral truth, thus striving for perfection in your integrity, honor, and charity?

...Catholic leadership is both the art and the science

- Do you practice and promote the ten Catholic leadership principles, thus providing yourself with a firm and static base from which to develop your leadership skills?
- Do you understand that the application of the leadership principles is meant to be fluid and adaptive to diverse situations, thus giving priority to some principles in certain situations and priority to other ones in different circumstances?
- Do you practice the leadership principles without rigidly binding yourself to them, thus balancing both the art and the science that true leadership requires?

...of guiding, shepherding, and managing

- Do you guide those that you lead, thus leading from the front when the situation calls for it, thereby forging and clearing a path towards the goal that you seek?
- Do you shepherd your flock, gently and with great care, herding them when the situation calls for it, thereby marshalling those around you to lead and guide themselves?

- Do you honestly manage and ably administer those that you lead, thus promoting the welfare of your subordinates and ensuring the efficiency and effectiveness of your entire group?

...other free-willed persons

- Do you remember that those individuals that you lead are free-willed persons, and thus must be respected and treated as such?
- Do you note that the leadership of free people must necessarily be earned, not expected, thus meaning that you must cultivate and earn deference, not merely anticipate it?
- Do you see your subordinates as the human beings that they are, not mere tools to be used for your own purposes?

...towards created and sustained goals, aims, and an overall Catholic vision

- Do you, as a leader, establish the goals, aims, and vision for your team, thus providing direction and purpose to their efforts?
- Do you, as a leader, contemplate, assess, and conscientiously choose your goals and aims with wisdom and forethought, thus ensuring that you are seeking a worthy and noble goal?
- Do you, as *the* leader, hold fast to the goals, aims, and overall Catholic vision that you have chosen, even when those around you have fallen prey to fear and uncertainty?

...without solely or explicitly relying on visible authority or coercive power

- Do you rely on just your authority to establish your leadership, or do you cultivate the respect and trustworthiness necessary to lead without explicit authority or power?

- Do you substitute power for true leadership, thus not actually leading your followers, but rather just driving them forward like a slave-driver whipping his human chattel?
- Do you believe that if you dropped all vestiges of official authority and sanctioned power, your subordinates would still follow you as their leader?

...God willing.

- And finally, do you remember that though a leader you may be, a follower of God you always are, and thus you must always hope that it is ultimately His will that is done, not yours?

In addition, above and beyond just extrapolating key questions from our definition of Catholic leadership, we must also ask further questions, this time relating to the ideas surrounding our understanding of Catholic leadership styles.

Loving Leadership

- Do you examine leadership situations properly and accurately in order to determine if a loving style of leadership is best suited to the particular situation that you find yourself in?
- When the situation calls for it, do you actually practice an active and loving leadership style?
- Do you truly demonstrate a deep and strong love to those subordinates that are inexperienced, uncertain, and need your assistance and active guidance?

Faithful Leadership

- Do you examine leadership situations properly and accurately in order to determine if a faithful style of

leadership is best suited to the particular leadership situation that you find yourself in?
- When the situation calls for it, do you actually practice a trusting and faithful leadership style?
- Do you truly demonstrate a secure and trusting faith to those subordinates that are experienced, sure in their skills, and competent?

All these questions, regardless of whether they are formally contemplated (as presented) or just informally considered in some other less rigorous format, must be unflinchingly faced and bravely answered. These are the questions, many though they may be, that challenge every Catholic leader. They are the questions that push every Catholic leader towards success. And they are the questions that will allow you, as a Catholic leader, to establish a firm understanding of what Catholic leadership needs to be, while simultaneously providing you with the means through which you can view and judge the advancement and development of your own leadership skills. For it is through the answering of these questions, and then honestly assessing those same answers, that we can be informed as to what our current leadership level is. And it is also through the answering of these questions, and then honestly assessing how many we can answer affirmatively, that we can determine how effective our leadership actually is. Finally, it is through answering these questions not only affirmatively, but rather with greater and stronger affirmation, confidence, and assurance, that we can gauge our growth as Catholic leaders, thus leading us closer and closer to the leadership ideal that every Catholic leader should seek. These questions—and others like them—are, therefore, an invaluable means for self-assessment and self-evaluation. They must be used, for they are such a valuable leadership tool that to not make use of them would literally be a sin!

Now, at the end of things, we come to a close. Together, we have taken a journey through the vast and various aspects and elements that surround the perennial topic of leadership. We have, furthermore, tied general concepts concerning leadership to Catholicism itself, developing the specific idea of *Catholic leadership,* and thoroughly exploring all that this idea entails for the Catholic leader. Finally, we have explored the means and the methods by which we can examine our own leadership skills, and the questions that must be asked in order to develop those Catholic leadership skills to a greater and deeper level. All the tools are thus in place. All the necessary skills have been described. And all the ideas have been presented. Go forth, therefore, and lead, yet do not simply lead, but lead well, always striving for perfection. Go forth, and be the outstanding leader that you most certainly can be, yet do not simply be a leader, but be a *Catholic* leader. And go forth, in the end, with the blessing and strength of the Lord Jesus Christ in this most noble and vital quest. Godspeed!

www.ingramcontent.com/pod-product-compliance
Lightning Source LLC
Chambersburg PA
CBHW031247290426
44109CB00012B/474